ABOVE Australia

A SALUTE TO OUR CITIES

Ansett.
B

ABOVE
Australia

A SALUTE TO OUR CITIES

Photography by Leo Meier

Text
by Keith Dunstan, Ross Gates, Robert Haupt, Nancy Keesing,
Hugh Lunn, Chris Milne, David Nason and Hugh Schmitt

URE SMITH

SYDNEY • HONG KONG • CHICAGO • LONDON

Design and Art Direction: Tony Gordon
Project Coordinator: Sheena Coupe
Production: Gary Baulman
Additional Photography: George Hall

First published by Weldons Pty Ltd 1985
Reprinted by Ure Smith 1990
a division of Kevin Weldon & Associates Pty Limited
372 Eastern Valley Way, Willoughby, NSW 2068, Australia

National Library of Australia Cataloguing-in-Publication Data

Meier, Leo, 1951–
Above Australia: a salute to our cities.

ISBN 0 7254 0804 9

1. Cities and towns — Australia. 2. Cities and towns — Australia — Pictorial works. 3. Australia — Aerial photographs. 4. Australia — Description and travel — 1976 — I. Dunstan, Keith, II. Title.

994.06'3

Typeset in Australia by Phototext, Sydney
Printed in Singapore by Kyodo-Shing Loong Printing Pte Ltd

URE SMITH

PARMELIA HILTON

Contents

Photo captions for preceding pages

FRONT COVER: *Exhibition Buildings, Melbourne*
PAGES 2–3: *Brisbane*
PAGES 4–5: *Sydney*
PAGES 8–9: *Darwin*
CONTENTS PAGES: *Perth*
PAGES 12–13: *Canberra*
THIS PAGE (Above): *Hobart*

Introduction

IT is one of the ironies of Australia's development that for so long our folk heroes have been country dwellers: bushrangers and drovers, squatters and shearers, diggers and swaggies. Despite this rural mythology, Australia has been, since the beginning of white settlement, an urban society. Those who were exiled to its shores, those who flocked to its goldfields, those who survived the long voyage in search of a better future — most were of the firm belief that their future lay in the towns and cities of Australia, not in its alien and frightening bush. The bush was eerie and dangerous, its hazards, known and imagined, too overpowering for those who had come from the teeming cities of Britain and Europe.

So they stayed in the fledgling colonial seaboard cities where, despite differences in climate, in building materials and in landscape, they tried to recreate the places they remembered as 'home'. From stone and brick they constructed government buildings, banks and stores. These were the symbols of security and progress, the visible signs of success and development. With their homes they were prepared to be more flexible, adapting the styles of Europe to suit the climate and materials of Australia.

And so the cities grew, each colonial capital serving as a centre of government, business, finance and administration. Relentlessly they moved outward — land was cheap and plentiful then — to create the suburban sprawl which is so apparent today as one approaches an Australian capital from the air. Houses and industries followed — and sometimes preceded — the roads and railway lines which radiated from the city centre, creating an intricate pattern, sometimes carefully planned, more frequently carved out and developed in the quickest possible time and at the lowest possible cost.

Although most of Australia's capitals had common beginnings and shared similar patterns of growth and development, they now display a remarkable diversity of character and appearance. While due in large part to such physical factors as climate, setting and landscape, this variety is also a reflection of the backgrounds, interests and aspirations of the people who live in them. Each city has its own characteristic tone, from the brash hedonism of Sydney to the brisk efficiency of Canberra, from the easygoing tropicality of Darwin to the cool formality of Melbourne, from the stately elegance of Adelaide to the subtropical lushness of Brisbane, from the dynamism of Perth in the west to Hobart's small-town charm in the south.

Above Australia *is a tribute to all these cities, and to those who built them and live in them. Like the cities themselves, this book reflects the rich diversity of Australian society.*

Sydney

NANCY KEESING

SHARP
SHARP
SENTRY
Australian Eagle

HILTON
PHILIPS

Pages 16 – 24: *Sydney is a city of potent symbols. The harbour was always there, its many inlets probing the land to create hundreds of kilometres of beautiful foreshores. Then came the Bridge, spanning that harbour from north to south. Later came the Opera House, its billowing sails a magnified reflection of hundreds of harbour craft.*

Below: *Sydney's latest symbol, Sydney Tower, soars above the Centrepoint complex in the city's business heart.*

THE BLACK STUMP is what Sydneysiders call the charcoal-grey State Office Block building in Macquarie Street. The windows of its reception area on the 31st floor yield wonderful views of the city and harbour. There I stood one night admiring the lights of cars crossing the Harbour Bridge to the big new buildings of North Sydney; the burnished tops of the Opera House sails; patterns of light from windows, roads and harbour ferries. Reflections of light at all times of day make of Sydney's harbour an enormous ever-changing opal. A well-known conservationist stood beside me. 'Isn't this one of the world's great views,' I exclaimed. 'I'm sure it was *once*,' she said sourly, 'but that' — and she arced her glass of sherry around the windows — 'is all man made.'

Of course it is; and I admire my city for the human vision, history and achievement that have made it great. My city. I was born here. I've lived and worked near the harbour for most of my sixty years. I loved Sydney when it was a low-roofed town of warm stone and brick; I love it now when its high-rise towers make a very different outline on the sky.

The older parts of town and the old, and older, buildings that survive speak to me of the history I inherited and much of my own history too. Today's pedestrian malls, plazas and parks, the paved spaces that surround new buildings, and the great towers themselves, affirm the present and the future. The tall gilded thrust of Centrepoint is a symbol of creation, life, fertility — and fertility of imagination. And determination. When the Centrepoint tower was barely begun I sat in a bus. Behind me two men talked loud and clear. One was an elderly architect, the other a middle-aged engineer. They explained to each other's satisfaction precisely why the huge structure never could and never would work. They prophesied that if it was perchance completed, anyone visiting it would be seasick from its swaying. Just look at it, and from it, now.

Where would Sydney be without its 'knockers'? (In Australian parlance a knocker belittles, grumbles or cries woe.) They impel the rest of us to 'show them'. Certainly Sydney's earliest knockers had justification for pessimism. A gaol is a gaol, and a beautiful prison, rather than one built of thick stone, might have a special poignancy. Our earliest forebears witnessed magnificent surroundings before man changed contours and tamed natural wildness, but none of them could afford the luxury of sentimentality. Exiled at the extreme of the known world on the fringe of a land not yet known at all, they felled trees and hewed sandstone to shelter themselves. They had poor and insufficient food and a meagre water supply.

Ætna
TAA

Sydney's city parkland, adjacent to the city centre: Hyde Park (left) *is a seventeen-hectare retreat; the Anzac Memorial is in the foreground. Across historic Macquarie Street are the Domain and Royal Botanic Gardens* (above). *St Mary's Catholic Cathedral in the foreground is a large and imposing Gothic Revival church designed by colonial architect William Wardell.*

Life for the earliest settlers, bond or free, was wretched and often brutish. Fortunately Arthur Phillip, the founding governor, and most of his successors in the colony's first sixty years, were men of vision and determination. So, too, were many of the early settlers including an increasing and increasingly influential group known as Emancipists — convicts who had earned their freedom.

Fortunately too, when permanent buildings first appeared, English architecture was dominated by beautiful, classical, simple Georgian styles. The city that began to take shape owed a great deal to several early architects, one of whom was the famous Francis Greenway, an ex-convict. Unfortunately there was no town planner. Sydney streets meandered all over its narrow, rocky and often steep site like Brown's cows and, indeed, many of them began as the tracks and short cuts created by people and cattle. On the skyline windmills — our first tall buildings — were landmarks.

Old and new but both distinctively white. The Sydney Opera House (left) *caused a storm of controversy when Joern Utzon's design was selected from an international competition. It was opened in 1973. The crenellated Conservatorium of Music* (right) *was originally designed by Francis Greenway as stables for a never-built Government House.*

Early Sydney was a raffish, and sometimes wicked, place. It was not only a prison, but an increasingly important sea-port, especially for ships engaged in whaling and sealing whose operations greatly expanded at the beginning of the nineteenth century. Until 1833 these were Australia's chief primary industries. Some visitors to Sydney commented on the stench of boiling blubber that hung like a miasma over the city despite government attempts to confine whale treatment works to the then remote north-western reaches of the harbour. Many whaling ships were built locally; others sailed down to southern waters from America. Pubs, taverns and brothels proliferated in the Rocks area and a bit later around the wharves of Woolloomooloo Bay.

While the riff-raff of the Rocks roistered and respectable citizens went to live elsewhere if they could, a very interesting example of the effect of a better environment was seen in Sydney and more widely in its hinterland. This was not designed as an 'experiment' and the environmental school of psychologists would not emerge until much later. The first generation of children born in the colony was growing up. Some were offspring of free settlers and the military and marine guards of the gaol, whose consorts were often convict women; many more were born to convict families.

No one had prophesied much good for the Currency (native-born) lads and lasses, but the children of the colony were a wonder to everyone. Surgeon Peter Miller Cunningham, who had made four journeys to New South Wales as surgeon-superintendent on convict transport vessels, marvelled to see how they shot up like cornstalks and overtopped their parents by inches. They had clear skins and strong limbs, swam like dabchicks and were usually quick to learn. They were the more astonishing by contrast with the pockmarked, rickety, ignorant, besodden wretches who bred them and for whose progeny no one had forecast any good at all.

Redevelopment plans are underway for the western part of the city (right) *now a jumble of freeway approaches, wharves and little used goods yards. The new Entertainment Centre* (below) *is part of this refurbishing.*

PHOTO GEORGE HALL

HILTON
NZI

Many parents were unmarried: sometimes because they lived in remote areas where clergy were seldom seen; sometimes because, like the Catholic Irish, no priest of their faith yet ministered in the colony. Bastard or not, few of the beautiful children had any education at all: they started work as soon as they were old enough to help on farms or take city jobs. Paradoxically, children of very poor families, victims of dire social problems, or delinquent children had some education at institutions like the Female School of Industry. Richer people paid school fees or employed tutors or governesses. From 1806 onwards there was a proliferation of dame schools in Sydney, but private school fees were far beyond the means of ordinary working folk.

From 1799 to 1845 there was a Government House at Parramatta and it was chiefly used by successive governors. The Parramatta River flows into a north-western reach of the harbour and until adequate roads were built this was the colony's chief link with the farming lands that supplied its food.

A road, parts of which are still called Pittwater Road, once linked the 'new' farms at Pittwater with the Parramatta River. Its remnant serves suburbs today. Some of the oldest surviving warehouses in Sussex Street were built for this river trade and later used for coastal cargo ships. Many of them have been cleaned, restored and recycled to present-day usefulness as offices, shops, galleries, and again display the skills of convict stonemasons and bricklayers and the vision of their designers.

Sydney's population increased markedly in the early 1830s and faster following the gold discoveries of the 1850s. During and after the 1880s further growth occurred with new suburban development and subdivision and improved networks of railways and other public transport.

The first gold discovery in New South Wales to be publicly announced was in February 1851, and the following July a gold discovery was announced in Victoria. Many Australian fortune hunters who had journeyed to the Californian diggings returned home; gold seekers from all over the world flocked to both colonies; gold rushes opened up back country, built roads, established towns and made cities rich. 'Marvellous Melbourne' mushroomed from tents to substantial houses and buildings in a few short years in the 1850s, but Sydney, founded some sixty years before that, was already a place of substance and substantial buildings. In Sydney the ornate Italianate architecture that gold financed rose beside older Georgian-style buildings but did not always replace them.

Erasmus Darwin (grandfather of Charles, the naturalist) never saw Sydney but in 1789, a year after its first settlement, he wrote a strangely prophetic poem about it. '*There*, the proud arch, Colossus-like bestride Yon glittering streams, and bound the chasing tide . . .', exclaimed Darwin, though it would be another 143 years before the Sydney Harbour Bridge was completed and opened.

Work on the Sydney Harbour Bridge began in 1923, the year I was born, and finished in 1932. It was very much a part and shape

Right: *Anzac War Memorial, Hyde Park, designed by Bruce Dellit and completed in 1934, is a fine example of Art Deco style amid the city towers.*

Below: *The sleek lines of the 65-storey tower of the MLC Centre dominate this view. Designed by Harry Seidler & Associates, the complex was opened in 1978.*

PHOTO GEORGE HALL

of my childhood, for I slept on the westward balcony of a house in Darling Point, and from its rail, or sitting up in bed, I looked over the hump of Elizabeth Bay, beyond the naval base at Garden Island, clear to spectacular sunsets or approaching storms — and to the bridge. Gradually it grew, so that first the two arcs of the arch crept together across the sky and, after they joined, vertical hangers, supporting the ever-lengthening deck, descended.

The harbour and its sounds were always with me. In misty or rough weather foghorns shrieked and sobbed through my dreams. When the wind blew from the north it carried the roar of lions from Taronga Park zoo. Trams were our transport by land and ferries by water. Sometimes my father hired a rowing boat and took us fishing from Double Bay or Rose Bay or Watson's Bay. We learned to swim in harbour baths and I first rode a pony on the beach at Double Bay. The sounds of horses still clip-clopped through our days. The milkman's cart arrived near dawn with a thud of patient hooves and a clatter of household billies being filled from a big milk container fitted with a spigot. A bit later the baker arrived. His horse often had its face stuck into a nosebag of tasty chaff which it chewed as it went from house to house while the baker carried his basket of loaves to each back door.

The Chinese 'vegetable John' had a very Chinese-looking cart, covered by a horizontal matting awning. The clothes-prop man came by every few months calling 'clo props'; sellers of rabbits yelled 'Rabbit-oh! Fresh rabbits!'; buyers of empty bottles from their carts yelled 'Bottle-oh! Any emmy bo-ulls?', and so on.

Some people lament that the old street cries of Sydney are no longer heard; I enjoy the new ones. Once — before cars were practically universal — bakers, butchers, fishmongers, grocers brought their wares to our back door for us to make our choices. The supermarket is our back door now, and the shopping complex is where you hear present-day street cries magnified a hundredfold by portable microphones. The Chinese vegetable John no longer, each Christmas, presents his customers with delicious ginger in syrup in a delicate jar; instead chain stores tempt, and pretend to reward us, with bingo cards and chances for a trip to Timbuctoo.

Sydneysiders are great gamblers and our twin penchants for sport and gambling manifested themselves early. Our first racecourse was in what is now Hyde Park; it was cleared for a race meeting in 1810. It was also the venue for early cricket matches. The first recorded race meeting was held at Parramatta a few months before the Hyde Park event and the first race was won by a horse called Parramatta from a horse called Belfast. 'The proceedings of the day', according to one contemporary account, 'were enlivened by cock-fighting, wheelbarrow racing, and jumping in sacks'. A publican gave enough calico to make a chemise for a prize 'to be run by three vestals of the currency order'.

Our forebears would bet on anything: a man leaping over three horses (1832); men running backwards; men rolling from one inner

Sydney is among Australia's busiest ports and much of the harbour foreshore around the city is given over to wharves and shipping. The docks of Darling Harbour (above) *are close by the historic Rocks area* (right), *its rows of terraces now split by the Bridge approaches.*

suburban pub to its neighbour hostelry. And, in 1845, they gambled on a real puzzler: at the Woolpack hotel in Petersham near the city, 'a wager was laid that a man would go one mile without touching the ground, and would not be drawn or ride on horseback'. The feat was accomplished on one of the earliest bicycles imported to Australia.

On the harbour there were sailing and rowing races, official and impromptu. The first Sydney regatta was in 1827. Swimming as a sport came later; the first championship swimming race was in the Domain baths in 1846. But swimming was forbidden in daylight hours on many beaches and men and women did not swim together unless they had access to a remote beach where the wowsers couldn't see them. Early in this century those laws were repealed and Sydney women swimmers like Annette Kellerman, Fanny Durack and May Wylie first astonished the locals and then, before World War I, made international reputations. Surfing, too, became popular early in this century. The cumbersome neck-to-knee costumes worn by both sexes until the 1920s may seem a far cry from the near-nudity on today's beaches but no doubt some brave spirits managed to get round the laws of the day.

Getting around, and evading, laws are traditional Sydney 'sports' too, and are closely allied to a dislike and distrust of police. This attitude was established nearly as early as first settlement because the Night Watch, and the police force that evolved from it, were chiefly staffed by convict and ex-convict constables who, by accepting these jobs, contravened one of our sacred unwritten rules: 'Thou shalt not dob in another person'.

In my city the wilderness is tamed, but never far away. While I was writing this my morning newspaper — the *Sydney Morning Herald*, founded in 1831 — reported a sighting of a humpback whale and her calf off a harbour landmark called the Sow and Pigs. They swam on towards the Opera House. I've seen seals in the harbour, and a sea lion near the bridge at Pyrmont, and more big sharks than I care to count. Our gardens are visited by tiny blue wrens; brilliant rosella parrots; raucous white cockatoos; omnivorous currawongs that indiscriminately devour flowers, fruit, and whatever small creature crawls or flutters; magpies; and a kookaburra that laughs merrily as it rides round on my rotary clothes hoist. (A great Sydney feature is the ubiquitous rotary clothes hoist!) We watched two noisy miners dive-bombing a Siamese cat clear down our side path and on up the road; they tackle currawongs, too. Possums are plentiful wherever there are tall trees. Frogs croak, crickets chirp, cicadas drum and bellow. Geckoes climb brick walls and, bless them, eat spiders, including the poisonous redbacks that lurk in sheltered corners; a stout, lethargic blue tongue lizard emerges from beneath the verandah to feast on snails. Everyone is wary of dangerous funnel-web spiders, but otherwise city dwellers have little to worry about. Snakes are still found in outer suburbs, but not in near-city ones and the fox that was allegedly seen not long ago in William Street — itself a thoroughfare notable for some

Port Jackson, described by Arthur Phillip as 'the finest harbour in the world, in which a thousand sail of the line may ride in perfect security', is today home to all manner of vessels, from pleasure yachts moored at Rushcutters Bay (right) *to workaday tugs and container ships* (above).

pretty foxy ladies — must surely have escaped from captivity somewhere. One can hardly imagine today an incident such as the one that occurred in March 1788 when an emu 'ran through Sydney and was shot. It stood 7 feet, 4 inches high'.

Taronga Park has excellent collections of Australian fauna, including emus and koalas descended from those that once were native to this area. For generations the zoo has been one of the city's traditional venues for a day out with the kids. You can drive there, or go there by bus, but the truly Sydney way to get to the zoo (or the beach at Manly) is by ferry. A Sydney ferry-boat laden with parents, picnic gear and excited children generates a kind of excitement that is unique; the throb of its idling engines accentuates the accelerating throb of an expectant crowd.

The enchantment of a ferry departing can only be matched by a steam train, and there are no steam trains any more. The underground railway system crisscrosses virtually the whole city centre and lines fan out, above ground, to suburban areas. Shops line the ramps that lead to underground stations and today most of these precincts link by tunnels and escalators to nearby shopping arcades and complexes. No one can miss seeing the skyscrapers that have altered the city's outline above ground, but the below ground 'revolution' has wrought great changes too. One could shop, eat and drink all day in central Sydney without ever seeing daylight or crossing a busy road.

Right: *The* Fairstar *is nudged into place at the Overseas Passenger Shipping Terminal, Circular Quay.*

Below: *Dawes Point, at the southern end of the Harbour Bridge. Some of the finger-like wharves of Walsh Bay are being refurbished and Pier One is now an entertainment, food and shopping complex.*

FIRE MUSEUM
FAIRSTAR

PHOTO GEORGE HALL

Sydney, of course, is not merely the city centre, or the area covered by its older suburbs. The name loosely refers to the area that stretches from the harbour headlands almost to the scarps of the Blue Mountains; from the southern rivers to Broken Bay. One of the glories of greater Sydney is that nearly all of it is beautiful, or close to places of beauty. It is only a walk, a bus ride or a short train trip from even its flattest and least interesting suburbs to beaches, parks, rivers and bush. The millionaires of Point Piper have marvellous views, but so do people who live in unpretentious houses and apartments around the harbour itself and up and down its tidal reaches, or along Botany Bay, or close to the northern and southern beaches. I think one needs to have experienced other cities to appreciate quite how fortunate Sydneysiders are.

At all seasons we live out of doors as much as we can. When one flies over suburbia a proliferation of backyard swimming pools look like unwinking blue eyes. Most of those yards also have a 'barbie', or barbecue; Australian slang is notable for abbreviations, often with the suffix 'ie', so that round those barbies, as well as eating steaks, we may munch 'bickies' and drink from 'tinnies'. Barbies vary from factory-made and elaborate to simple wire grids set over a few bricks. You don't need your own garden to enjoy outdoor pleasures, so at weekends and holidays families converge by car on popular beach or picnic places. They set up comfortable arrangements of portable chairs and tables and keep food and drink cool in insulated boxes.

Changing light; a changing view. Looking from Millers Point towards the Heads (above); *the city at dusk* (right); *and Fort Denison as night falls* (below). *This rocky harbour outcrop was fortified in 1857 as protection against Russian invasion at the height of Crimean War fever.*

HILTON
BARCLAYS
NORWICH
GOLD FIELDS
PIER ONE

AMP
2
3
4
5

QANTAS
HILTON
Martins
ROYAL

The glowing, streaming lights of Sydney: the city centre from Walsh Bay (pages 42–43); *the arching Bridge* (above); *North Sydney Olympic Pool* (left); *the Opera House* (above right); *around the Quay* (right); *and William Street, looking towards the city* (far right).

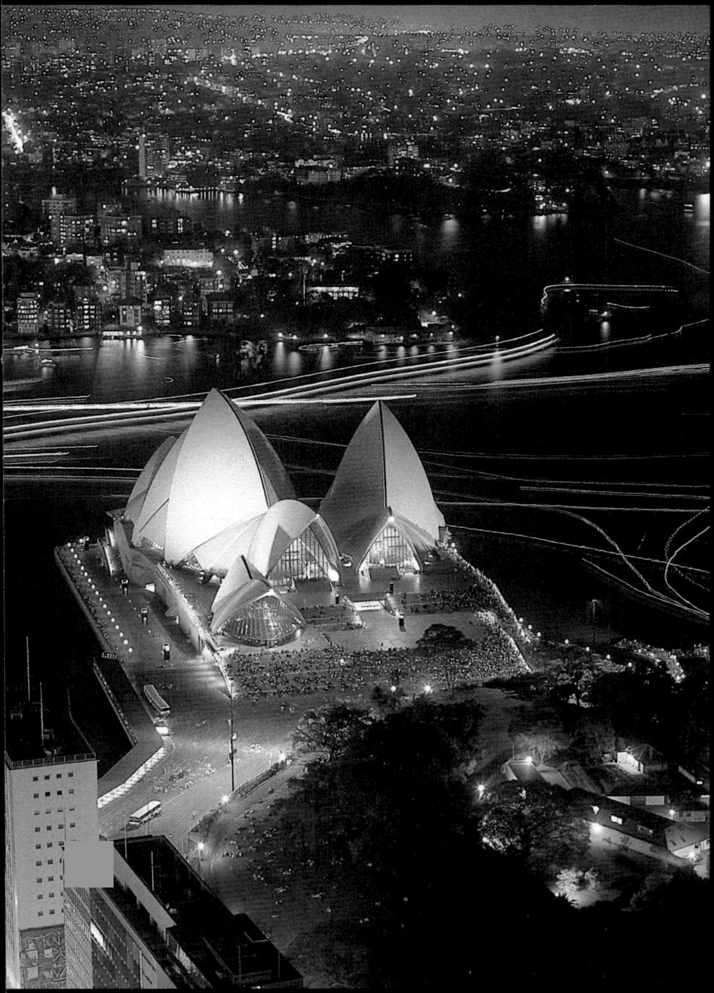

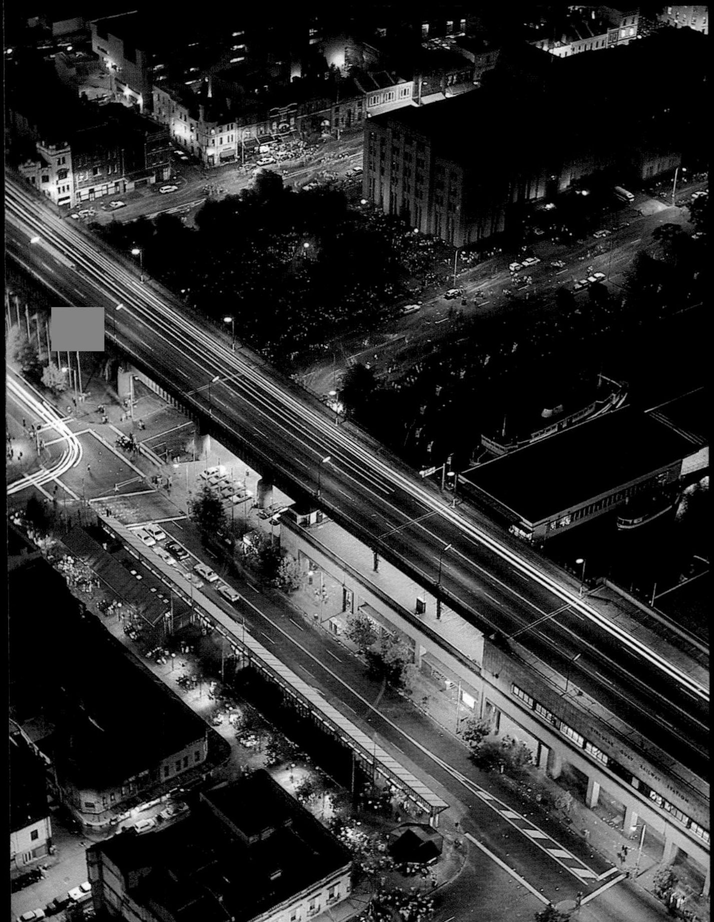

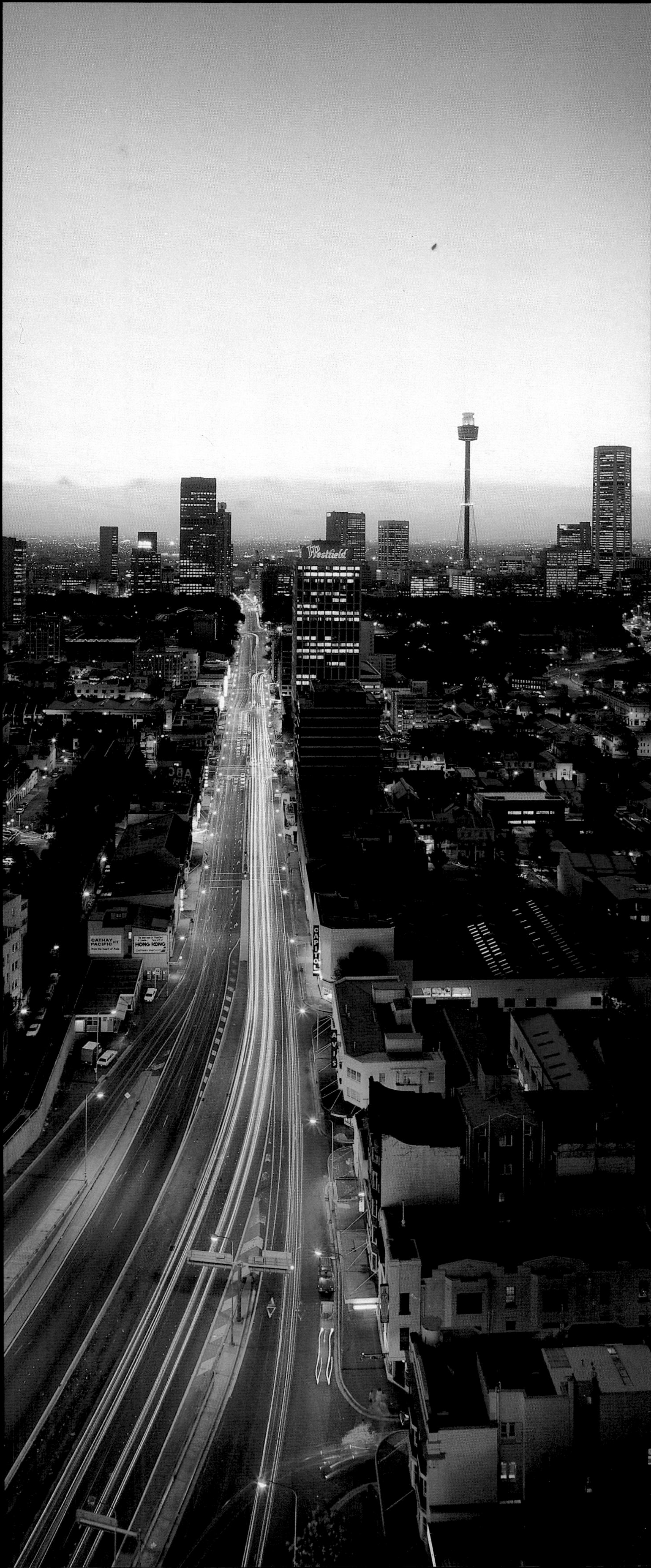
Westfield
CATHAY PACIFIC

By morning the city takes on different tones. The inner-city terraces reflect a gentle light; their inhabitants begin the daily round. William Street (below) *looks more subdued, with part of the Eastern Suburbs railway snaking past to its right and disappearing under the Domain.*

PASTICCERIA
ESPRESSO BAR
Telegraph

Morning: Eastern Suburbs commuters approach Kings Cross (left); *a quick cup of coffee in the morning sun* (above); *a welcome break after a hard night* (below); *the almost deserted streets of Darlinghurst* (right).

SYDNEY CITY MISSION
FIRE STATION

PHOTO GEORGE HALL

The rocky extremities of Port Jackson, parts of which have been incorporated into the Sydney Harbour National Park. Watsons Bay (above left) *with the infamous Gap, near South Head; North Head* (below left) *with the famous pines of Manly Beach to the left.*

At Nielsen Park a Middle Eastern family often picnics near our favourite patch of shade. While the young parents and children enjoy the waves some eight grannies and grandfathers relax and converse under a weeping fig tree, pouring frequent cups of Turkish coffee from a most beautiful brass coffee pot that bubbles over a spirit burner set on its own brass tripod. When the swimmers return they grill kebabs on a portable gas barbie and serve out tabouli and other marvellous-looking salads.

Except for the famous Sydney rock oysters the region has no foods that are unique to it. Restaurants, cafes and take-away shops reflect our multicultural food tastes offering dishes from China, Japan, Malaysia, India, France, Russia, Germany, Greece, Italy, Israel, Lebanon and many more. We buy recipe books from great displays in shops, and experiment with food, as well as aids and gadgets for its preparation.

Nothing and nowhere is perfect. Nearly all major libraries, museums and art collections are still in the city proper. Theatre has been more mobile, but vast areas of Sydney's hinterland are inconveniently far from its centres of history and culture. I reflect that when the Art Gallery, the museum in College Street, the State Library of New South Wales and the Botanic Gardens were established, the total population of the city was much less than the population of its major suburban centres today. Suburban libraries, galleries and other facilities may not be an adequate answer to the problem of providing all citizens with equivalent advantages.

Sydney has been called 'Sin City' and 'Tinsel Town'. Behind these derogatory names we suspect jealousy for a place that glitters with energy, events and entertainment.

The gabled Victorian cottages and double- or triple-storeyed terrace houses that are so notable a feature of our urban scenery chiefly date from the 1880s and 1890s when thousands of hectares of near-city land were subdivided for urban housing. The houses were often lavishly decorated with cast-iron lace, a fashion that was not universally approved! In 1893 the Engineering Association of New South Wales commented in its Proceedings: 'At the present time there is a term — "cast-iron impudence" — with its origin in the glaring and impudent manner in which cast-iron ornamentation is plastered over our buildings . . . almost 80 per cent of recent erections in the colonies rely on this stuff for appearance.'

How times change! Engineers, architects and handyman citizens who work at restoring and renovating old buildings now try to find genuine old iron lace or, failing that, use faithful reproductions of it — often in sprayed aluminium.

Landmark churches like St James in King Street and nearby St Mary's Cathedral, and a few other historic school and hospital buildings, are still used for their original purposes; at Sydney Grammar School, for instance, newer structures cluster around the graceful 1832 building erected for an even earlier school. Some structures, like the Old Mint and Convict Barracks in Macquarie Street, have been accurately repaired and restored outside and transformed into fine museums within. The whole area of Darling Harbour, where decayed railway lines and sheds sprawl over hundreds of hectares of near-city harbourside land, is to be turned into a splendid place of parks, restaurants and other facilities in time for Australia's Bicentenary — which will be my city's two hundredth birthday, too — in 1988.

The National Trust gives advice to people contemplating the restoration of Victorian and Federation (turn-of-the-century) houses. Some home owners achieve authentic results; the efforts of others are distinctly chi-chi but, at least, we are more prepared to preserve and recycle old buildings, wharves and houses than were our forefathers. Over past eras we lost too much to wreckers. Sometimes, though, we've been lucky. In 1959 Ray Lindsay, one of a notable family of Sydney artists, wrote to his brother Jack, who lives in England, about the Queen Victoria Market building. He called it 'a hideous Byzantine structure with an immense green dome. It still stands but there is frequent talk of tearing it down'. Fortunately it survived and is today being restored with particular care and splendour.

An excellent way to rediscover one's city is through the eyes and responses of an overseas visitor. When Ursula le Guin, an American writer, visited Sydney in the 1970s she wanted to see the Opera House but not, she said, on a conducted tour. One morning we walked from Wynyard Park, past St Patrick's church in Grosvenor Street and on through the Rocks; then down to Circular Quay via Cadman's cottage, which was built in 1816 and is Sydney's oldest extant building. We paused at the little park on the western side of the Quay among squabbling seagulls, then strolled along the pathway past the ferry wharves. I showed Ursula the place where, if you peer over the railings, you can see the circular drain through which the Tank Stream still dribbles into the harbour. It was our first water supply, but was long ago covered by roads and buildings. At the Opera House we climbed the front steps and explored the public areas. Ursula admired the tapestries, waxed lyrical about the views, but said she'd dearly like to clamber over the sails. So we discovered some outside steps I'd never known existed, and clamber we did — like, as she said, flies on a magnificent sculpture. And, of course, that wonderful building under full sail is just that.

Over restorative coffee on the open area facing the harbour she talked so much of shape and form that I offered to show her some different kinds of sculpture. In the Botanical Gardens near Man o' War Steps is the statue called 'The Satyr' sculpted by Frank (Guy) Lynch with the fawn-like face of his brother Joe Lynch who was its model. Joe Lynch later fell from a ferry and drowned in the harbour. Kenneth Slessor, who wrote much poetry of Sydney, commemorated his drowned friend in his poem 'Five Bells'.

After that I led Ursula to an immense Moreton Bay fig tree to admire the shapes and buttresses of its trunk and roots. The shapes and textures of my city are very various.

PHOTO GEORGE HALL

Sydney's harbour and coastal beaches are perhaps its greatest asset. Each summer the beaches and waterways are thronged with enthusiastic devotees of water sport.

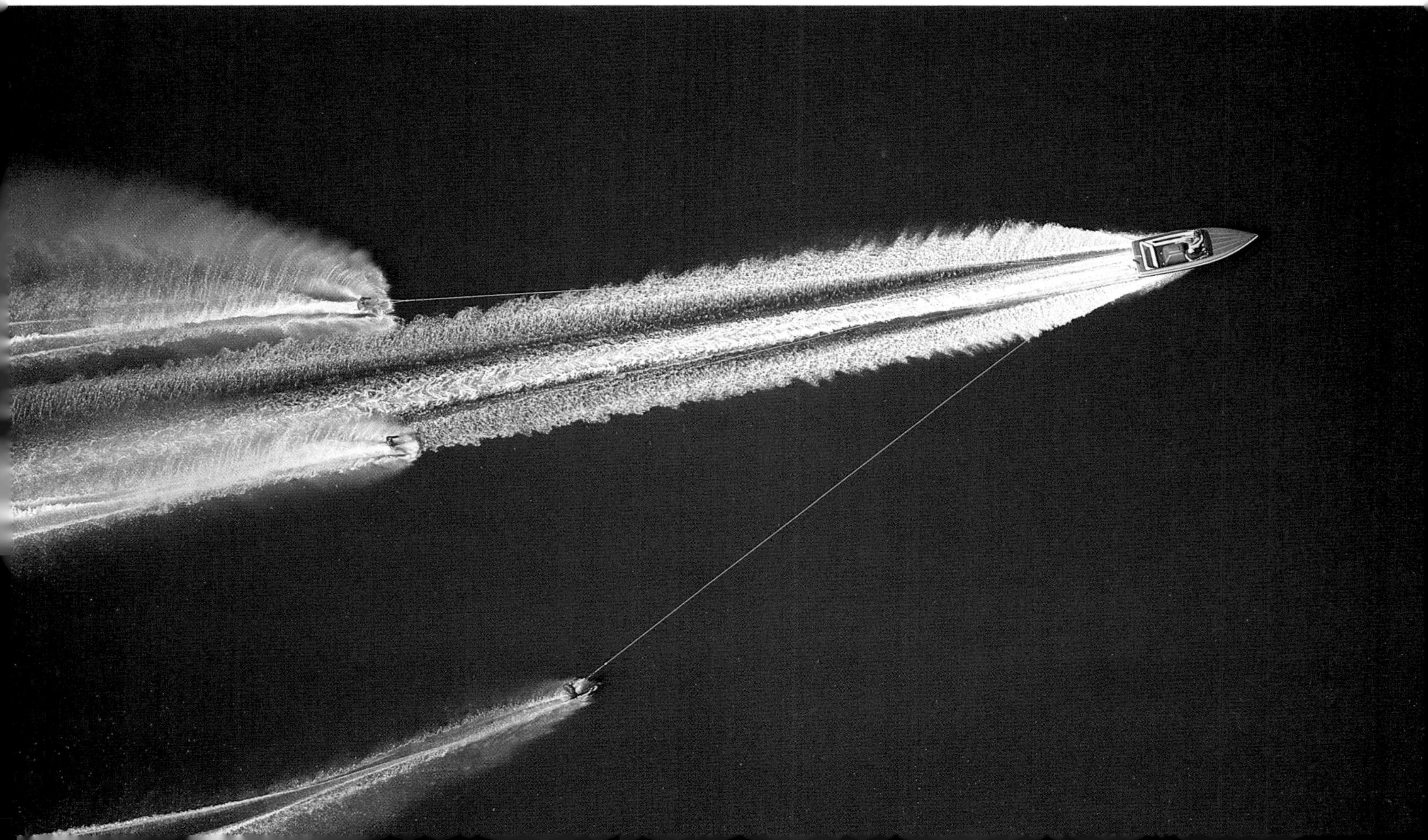

PHOTO GEORGE HALL

Above: *Relaxing by the sea at secluded Lady Bay, Sydney's first official nudist beach, just inside the harbour at South Head.*

Left and right: *Windsurfing, a relatively new and demanding sport, is rapidly gaining popularity on Sydney's waterways.*

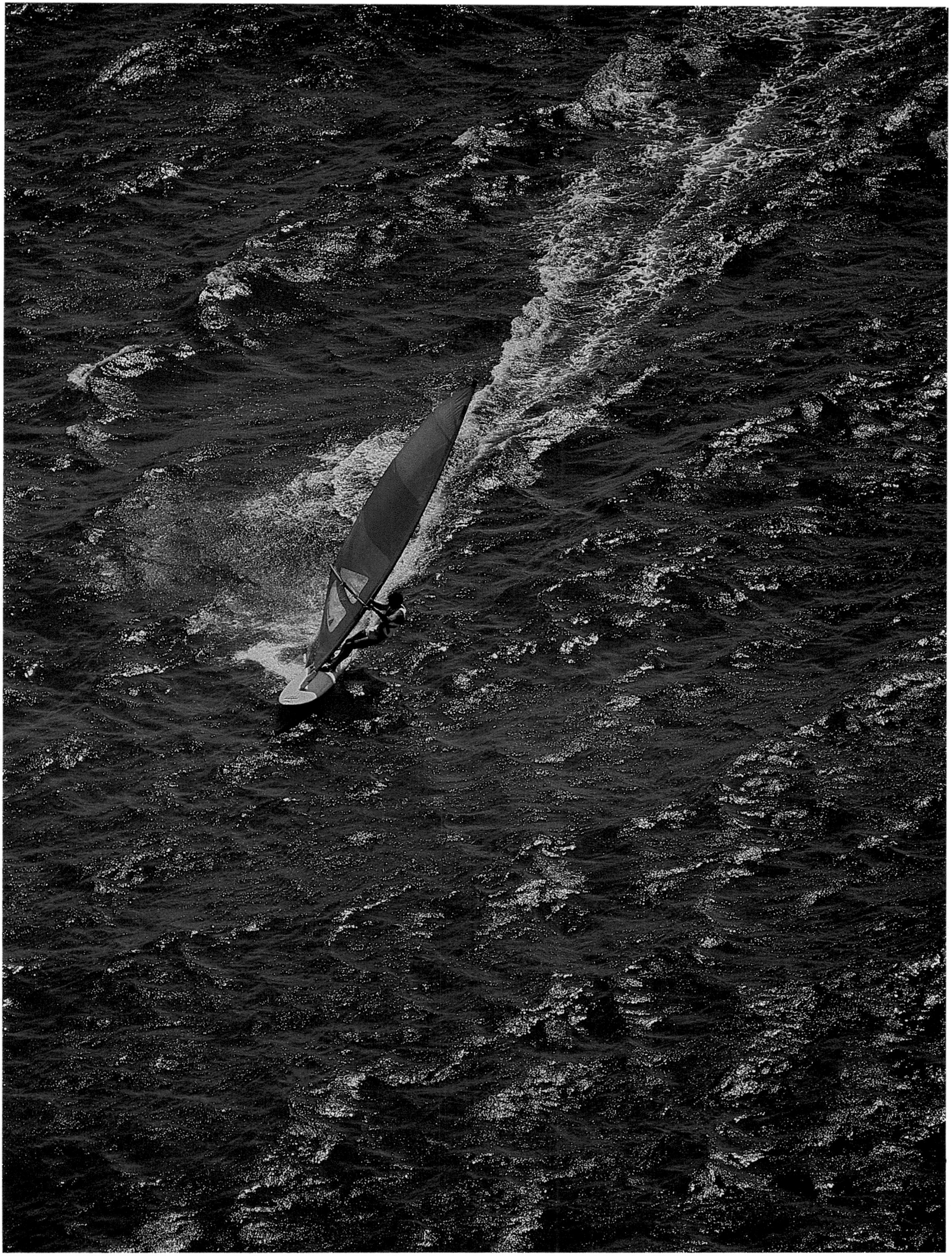

PHILIPS
Zurich
CLYDE
SONY

I'll finish with beginnings, for Sydney began long before 1788.

Even close to the city proper there are still legacies of the lives of countless generations of Aboriginal people spanning, perhaps, some forty thousand years. There are harbourside caves where fires have been lit and shellfish consumed over aeons, and mounds of shellfish shells nearby to depths of many metres. There are still, even in suburbs, a few remaining carvings on rock faces. In national parks there are large numbers of rock carvings and some caves whose walls carry the outlines of hand stencils. Sydney is a city of long memories.

Above: *In the shadow of the Bridge, the apartment blocks of Kirribilli, Luna Park and the North Sydney Olympic Pool.*

Left: *With its high-rise tower blocks and modern commercial buildings, North Sydney rivals the city proper as a centre of business activity. The idea of a bridge linking the north of the harbour with the south was first proposed in 1815 but it was not until 1932 that the Sydney Harbour Bridge was opened, joining Milsons Point in the north with Dawes Point in the south and making possible the rapid development of the north shore.*

Melbourne
KEITH DUNSTAN

THERE IS AN OLD SAYING that the key to Melbourne is simple. The great Carlton Brewery is at one end of Swanston Street; down the other end in St Kilda Road is the Shrine; the Melbourne Cricket Ground over to the left makes the third point of the triangle; the Anglican and Roman Catholic cathedrals are in between.

If you understand that lot, then you understand Melbourne.

Well that was true, almost. I grew up in the Melbourne of the 1930s. Sydney, we felt, was a wild, raffish, sort of place. Almost any sort of sin could take place in Sydney, whereas there was a sense of stolidity, immense security, in Melbourne.

The city was surrounded by a series of incomparably beautiful parks and gardens — always tidy, never a leaf out of place. The floral clock in St Kilda Road, composed of the correct seasonal flowers, reflected the purity of Melbourne.

The wowsers were completely in charge. The hotels closed at 6 p.m.; glasses were whipped off tables at 8 p.m. It was a sin to drink after dark. Sunday was a day of total purity: there was no sport; you weren't even allowed to play cricket in the parks.

Brian Fitzpatrick had my favourite quote. The Melbourne Sunday had a tranquillity, a pure beauty. Why, it was a work of art like the Winged Victory of Samothrace, the Two Minutes Silence, or *La Giaconda.*

The Melbourne Sunday was so astonishing it was a tourist attraction. The *New York Times*, the *Observer* in London, *Le Figaro* in Paris sent feature writers to do stories on it. There were no Sunday newspapers: it was a sin to produce a newspaper on a Sunday. The only establishment open, I think, was the zoo. It was all right to look at a gorilla on a Sunday.

When Stanley Kramer came here to make *On the Beach*, the film about the end of the world, it was perfect for scenes of streets totally devoid of humans.

Eating out was terrible. There were a few restaurants, mostly Italian: the Florentino, the Latin, the Society, the Ritz, Mario's . . . There were little Greek cafes in Swanston Street, Bourke Street and Russell Street. The specialty was steak'n'eggs or mixed grill. Always you used to get chips, a slice of tomato and lettuce cut up into streamers.

And we ate pies. Heavens, how we ate pies. We still do. Melbourne remains unquestionably the pie capital of the world. Indeed the Four'n'Twenty pie factory in Kensington on the edge of the Golden Mile, has the biggest, fastest pie machines anywhere. They have two machines which produce 3000 pies an hour. Australians eat 210 million pies a year, and Victorians are by far the most passionate pie lovers. Just to stand in that factory and gaze is an unbelievable experience: a great tide of pies, a moving ocean, passes before the eye.

Pages 58–59: *The skyline of Melbourne, looking to the south-west.*

Left: *The city centre, with the World Trade Centre in the foreground, on the banks of the Yarra.*

Below: *'Vault', a sculpture near the World Trade Centre, stands beside a conglomeration of railway tracks between Flinders Street and Spencer Street stations.*

Ah yes! In the thirties Anzac Day was the one true national day, when an enormous body of men, the returned Diggers, moved down Swanston Street to the Shrine. It was an honest holy day: no work, no sport; no one would dare desecrate it. Other institutions we revered were the Boat Race on the Yarra, the Grand Final, Test cricket at the MCG and the Melbourne Cup. We were convinced that Flinders Street Railway Station was the busiest in the world and that Collins Street was the world's loveliest city street.

That nice end, up by the Oriental Hotel and the Treasury building, we called the Paris End. How it ever won that title I don't know. Barry Humphries used to ask wistfully whether there was also a Melbourne end of the Champs-Élysées.

I am telling you all this, because there is practically no kin between the Melbourne of my youth and the Melbourne of today. In 1984 the Victorian government liberated the licensing laws. Already there were special licences to allow drinking to 3 a.m. on weekdays, but now on Sundays hotels could open from noon to 8 p.m. There was practically nothing on which you could not bet. In 1984 we won Footy TAB, which enabled us to bet on football. Before we could bet on horses and dogs; this enabled us to bet on humans as well.

From 1970 on there was a steady spread of massage parlours. In 1972 a government Chief Secretary began to wonder what sort of massage was conducted in these parlours. Melbourne seemed to have an extraordinary backache problem. In 1976 by official estimate Melbourne had 193 massage parlours and a police chief described us as 'the massage parlour capital of the world'. The establishments were in every suburb including the city. They had wonderful names such as Bubbles, Caesar's Retreat, Cloud 9, Pussycats and Peninsular Poppets. We even had one called 'Upstairs Downstairs' and I often wondered whether you could get massage from Lady Bellamy.

In 1984 the government by legislation stated that massage parlours from now had to be called brothels and they had to be registered by local councils. The wowser city was one of the first in the world to make prostitution legal. There were complaints that there was a massage parlour, very luxurious, in the old Paris End of Collins Street. 'Only one minute's walk from Parliament House', was the complaint. Why that made it worse than anywhere else is not entirely clear.

I live within fifty metres of Toorak Road, South Yarra. Up to ten years ago Toorak Road on a Sunday had the utterly correct Brian Fitzpatrick tomb-like qualities. Now it seethes. The old Stockdale bakery at the corner of Chapel Street is a vast fun parlour. Bookshops, hamburger houses, pizza parlours, ice-cream parlours, pubs, are all open and the scene is something to behold: males and females with heads as bald as ostrich eggs, faces painted white like Aboriginal tribesmen; others with spiked hair in vermilion, puce and various tasteful colours.

Honestly, in South Yarra and Chapel Street, Prahran, I have

Above and right: *The Shrine of Remembrance is the centre of a peaceful reserve adjacent to busy St Kilda Road, one of Melbourne's major arteries.*

Below: *Part of the Royal Botanic Gardens, thirty-five hectares of manicured parkland within the city.*

Travelodge

Above: *A panorama of the city: the Melbourne Cricket Ground is on the left; Government House and the Myer Music Bowl in the Domain in the centre.*

Far left: *Government House, first occupied in 1875.*

Left: *The Myer Music Bowl, a focal point for outdoor entertainment.*

seen more punks, more gays, more straight-out oddballs than even in Hollywood Boulevard, Los Angeles. The metamorphosis has been beyond belief.

There are now more than 300 licensed restaurants and 1800 BYOs. The title BYO, 'Bring Your Own', is a rich Australian phrase that was born in Melbourne. Many famous gourmets have been spellbound by the sight of Melburnians carrying their bags of liquor, and even casks, into restaurants which have this peculiar licence which does not allow them to sell liquor but does allow patrons to bring their own. Robert Carrier, the cookbook king, couldn't believe the BYO scene. He went out with his own little bag and was fascinated. The specially designed insulated BYO bag had its origin here; however a veteran campaigner prefers his battered Qantas or Pan American airways bag. You need a little style to hand it over with elegance to the head waiter, but as I write, I think back to the fifties when there were only half a dozen restaurants in the entire city where the prim authorities would allow us to drink wine. I have a wine-loving friend who flies to Melbourne every year from Los Altos, California. It is his idea of a perfect night out, being able to go to a good BYO. He adores to browse through the wine shops for several hours beforehand and make his own fastidious selection of the bottles he wants to take.

And Melbourne does have Australia's finest range of restaurants. I don't think there is any serious quibble about that. Indeed in forty years it has gone from zilch, steak'n'eggs, mixed grill nowhere to world class and far superior to most cities I know in the United States. I think with mouth watering love of Two Faces, Clichy, Fannys, Vlado's, Massonis, Frenchys, Fleurie, Glo Glo's, Filippos, Tsindos, Stephanies . . . Oh, I could go on and on.

Melbourne is now on a high, an entirely new mood. We have had many moods and an intense inferiority complex. We were always the most kickable, the most knockable of Australian cities. Our newspaper libraries have a plump file titled 'Melbourne — Criticism of'. Public relations firms know well that the easiest way for a visiting entertainer to make the front pages is to assault Melbourne for its vulgarity, ugly buildings, weather, lack of night life, dreary bay. The scar still hasn't healed from the day Ava Gardner described Melbourne as the ideal place to film the story of the end of the world. It was, although Ava Gardner denies she ever said it.

Yet, why this inferiority complex? The explanation goes back a long way, to Melbourne's rambunctious youth. In the 1870s and 1880s Melbourne was a city of brashness, excitement and self-confidence, bigger and more exuberant than Sydney. People had come here to escape from the restrictions, the dead customs, the class struggles of the old world, and they honestly believed the zest was here to create something superior. Bourke Street was a jolly gaslit marvel, the public buildings were astonishing for a city so young, and in 1889 we were bold enough to erect in Elizabeth Street the APA building, '150 feet high', which we were told was the tallest office building in the world.

Above: *Melbourne's suburban railway lines sweep into the city towards Flinders Street station* (centre left). *A view towards the port area.*

Right: *Like all Australia's capitals, Melbourne was established close to a potential commercial port. A view looking south to Port Phillip Bay.*

Just to give you some idea of the enthusiasm, in 1888 the city brought out a massive two-volume survey called *Victoria and Its Metropolis.* They thought God had selected Melbourne to lead the world and here was a city with an air of magic — 'The Star City of the South', 'Marvellous Melbourne'.

In 1892 came the bank crash and the worst depression Melbourne has known. Thousands were so desperate they took to the road. St Paul's Cathedral announced a Day of Public Humiliation, and the clergy called on the financiers to pray for forgiveness for their sins. The shock, the blow to confidence, was so profound Melbourne did not recover its boisterous image. Not, maybe, until now.

Building almost lapsed until the 1960s. What did we build between the two world wars? The Manchester Unity building, the Hotel Australia and very little else. The favourite topic for all visitors and commentators was Melbourne's appalling climate. Appalling indeed? Melbourne is closer to the equator than Madrid, Athens, Lisbon, all of France, most of Italy, and most of Sicily. Our position is the equivalent of, say, the middle of the Mediterranean. We are closer to the sun than most Greek islands. We get 657 mm of rain a year, compared with 1029 mm in Sydney and 1148 in Brisbane.

There are excellent reasons for the moods of Melbourne; people often wonder why we developed this superb sense of sin. It is a mistake to think that the great tidal wave of people who came to Victoria during the gold rush was composed entirely of roughnecks and remittance characters; many of them were good Methodists from Cornwall, splendid Presbyterians from Scotland.

Above right: *The law courts stand solid and elegant amid a rash of modern buildings.*

Below right: *Museum Station, on the corner of Latrobe and Swanston streets.*

Below left: *The symmetrical steel tracks of suburban railway lines crossing the Yarra.*

Below: *Melbourne Cricket Ground, the largest cricket arena in the world and scene of the 1956 Olympic Games.*

The Victorian Government Year Book of 1874 tells the whole fascinating story. We had 445 Anglican churches and 347 Roman Catholic, but there were 600 Presbyterian and 783 Wesleyans. What's more, as churchgoers, the Wesleyans outnumbered the Anglicans by more than two to one.

The great European migration of the 1960s changed all that. Melbourne with its availability of jobs scored a bigger percentage of migrants than any city. Prahran became one of the greatest Greek cities on earth and Carlton–Fitzroy had more Italians than almost any city in Sicily. The social change was profound. In 1976 the CSIRO made a survey and found that less than 70 per cent of people in the inner suburbs had been born in Australia. Fitzroy was the top migrant suburb with only 49 per cent Australian-born.

It wasn't just the change of eating habits; it was entire lifestyle. One of the lovely, almost untold stories is of the great Melburnian vintage which takes place every March, when the southern Euro-

Above left: *The Rialto rises to dominate the city skyline.*

Above: *Looking east along the Yarra, Melbourne's bridges are seen as a vital link in the urban network.*

Left: *Flinders Street Station and St Paul's Cathedral in the heart of the city.*

Fold-out pages 72–74: *Albert Park Lake, the city and the beginnings of the suburban sprawl.*

peans make their wine. Some make their wine in hand presses; some make it in the classic old-fashioned way by trampling the grapes with their feet in bathtubs.

Melbourne was always an extremely class-conscious city. Money and style were matters of immense importance. The school world was divided between those who went to the so-called public schools like Melbourne Grammar, Scotch College and Wesley and those who did not. Without exception all the public schools, including the well-to-do Catholic schools, were on the south side of the Yarra. The Yarra, narrow and muddy though it may be, was the complete class division.

All the best swimming beaches, all the best golf clubs, were on the south side. To the west and north-west there were Essendon, Footscray, Brunswick, Preston, Collingwood, Keilor. Decent enough, but if you had your eyes on glory and a seat on the board of BHP you didn't live there. Heidelberg was the exception; that is

LEGAL AND GENERAL

just over the Yarra. Sunbury also was good, for there you were close to the Rupert Clarkes.

This reached its peak during the conservative heights of the Malcolm Fraser federal elections. The Yarra was the perfect dividing line: Diamond Valley, Casey, Henty, Latrobe, Isaacs and Holt all went to the Liberals; across the water Scullin, Batman, Melbourne Ports, Gellibrand and Maribyrnong went soundly to Labor. This nut-brown stream was like a political Suez.

Comparisons between Melbourne and Sydney are fairly pointless, but there is a gallop on to prove which is the financial and cultural capital. At least until the 1960s Melbourne indisputably was the finance centre, but now it is more evenly balanced. The two biggest mining companies — BHP and CRA — are in Melbourne. So too are the headquarters for the two biggest retail houses — Myer and Coles. The biggest automobile companies — Ford and GMH — both belong in Melbourne. What's more, the city owns Elders-IXL, the biggest pastoral house and the biggest brewer.

Sydney, on the other hand has immense strengths in banking. Most of the international banks have their representatives in Sydney. Sydney is home for the Reserve Bank, the Commonwealth Bank, Westpac, AMP and CSR. On the culture scene, the Australia Council is based in Sydney, the Australian Opera is in Sydney; but the Victorian Opera is a mighty force, the Australian Ballet Company is in Melbourne and the Melbourne Theatre Company is by far the nation's largest drama entrepreneur.

Above: *High-rise office blocks dominate the skyline along the Yarra.*

Right: *Melbourne by day and night. Princes Bridge leads into the city past Flinders Street Station and St Paul's Cathedral.*

Fold-out pages 75–77: *As day ends, the world of commerce gives way to the different rhythms of Melbourne after dark.*

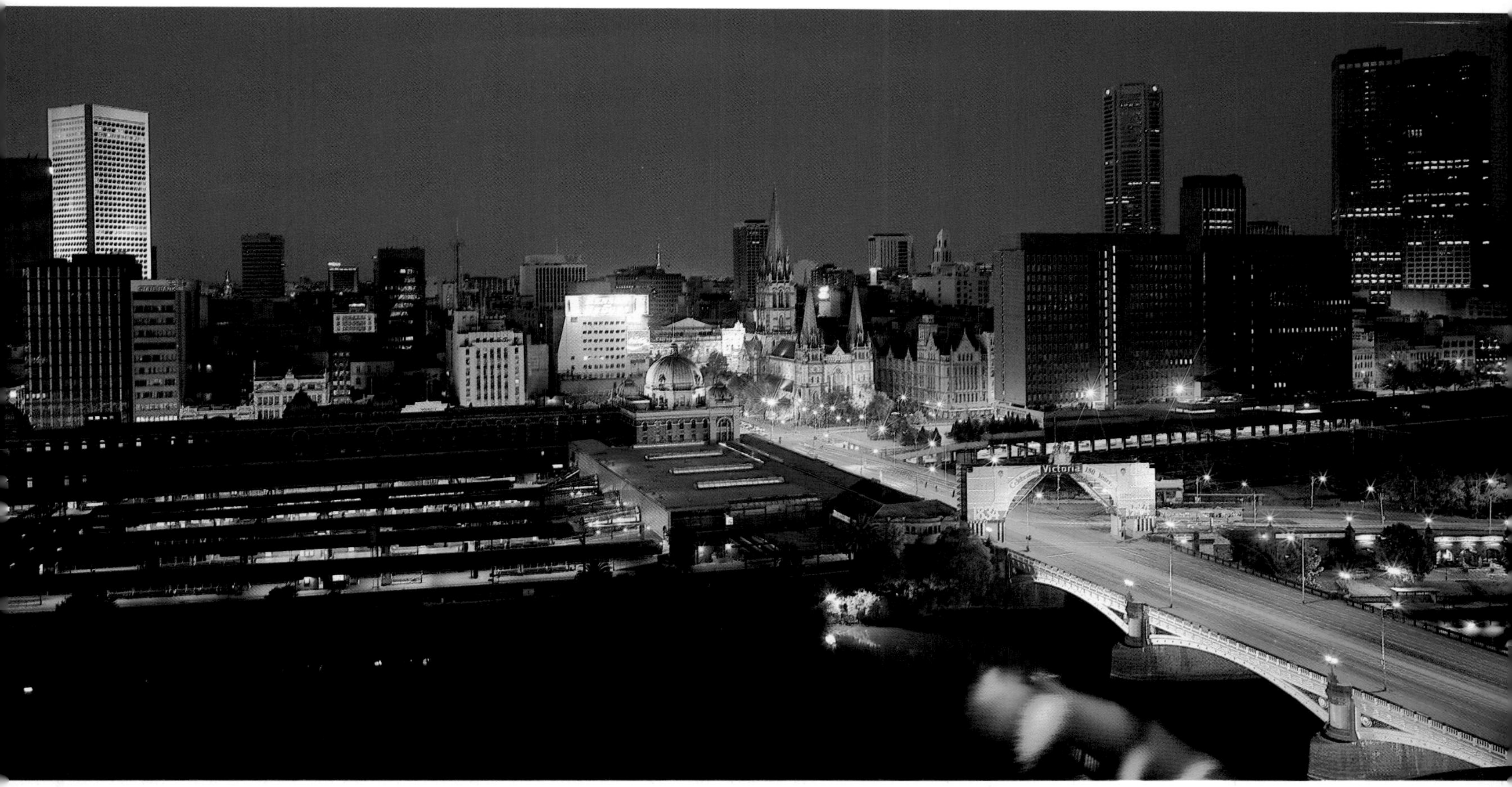
Victoria

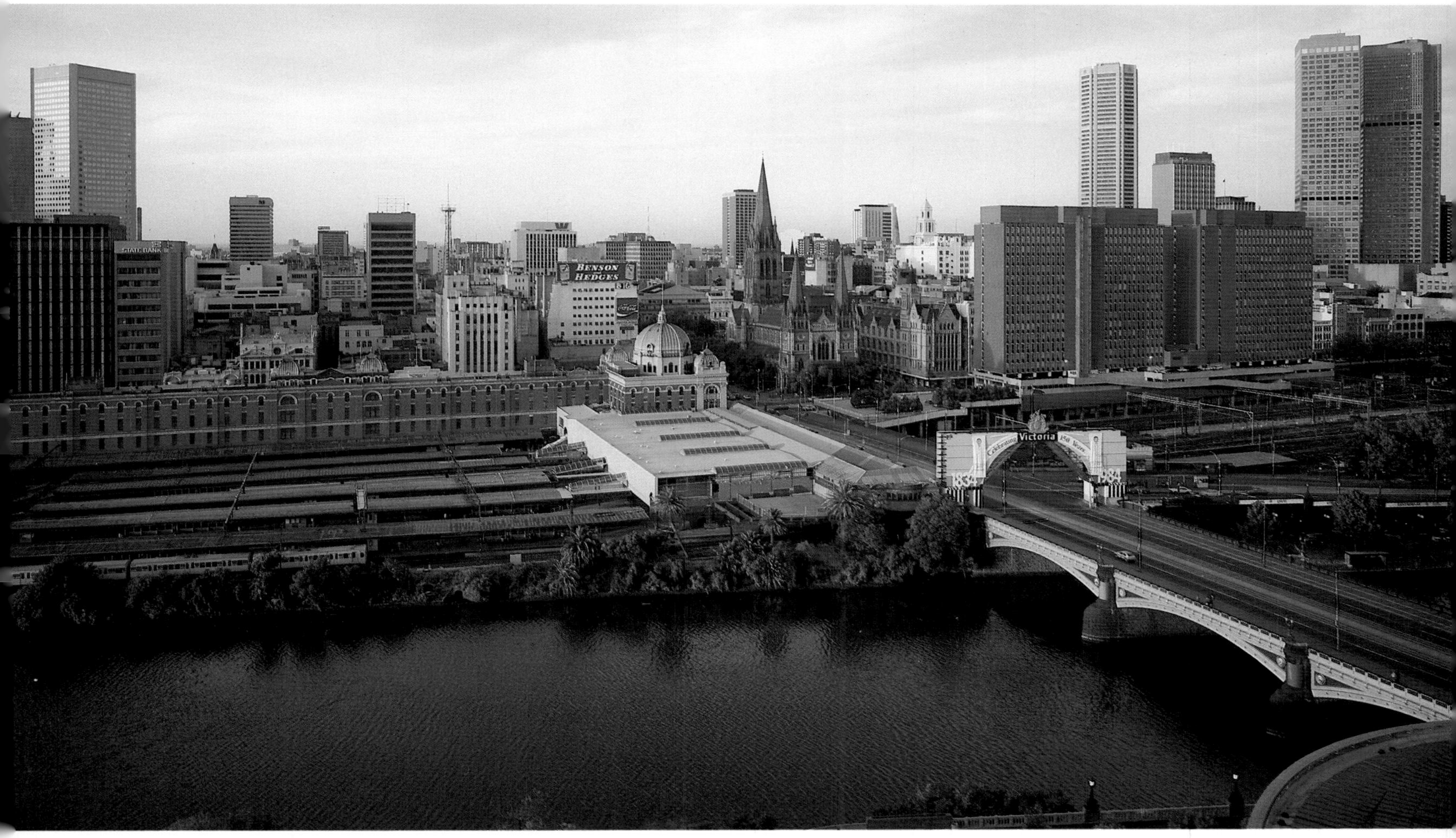
STATE BANK
BENSON
HEDGES
Victoria

Above: *The lights of Melbourne stretch north towards Tullamarine.*

Right: *The Arts Centre, opened in 1984, has quickly established itself as a city landmark.*

VICTORIA 150

Looking towards Port Phillip Bay. The World Trade Centre on the right, completed in 1983, is a commercial complex of offices, display centres

and restaurants. Nearby Batman Park houses 'Vault', the yellow abstract sculpture by Ron Robertson-Swann.

Oh yes, we move, we change; and unquestionably the most beautiful, wonderful thing that has happened in Melbourne this past decade has been the development of the Arts Centre. It came to its final completion only in November 1984 and for many it was like a dream — the culmination of twenty years of planning. I don't know of any complex quite like it. There is a beautiful art gallery, which we modestly describe as the finest in the southern hemisphere; there is a great concert hall; there is the State Theatre with huge stage and facilities as well as the Playhouse and a small intimate theatre called the Studio. It is all interconnected with parking space for several thousand cars and with restaurants, bars and shops.

The Concert Hall and the theatres have been successful beyond anyone's hopes. Night after night, they are filled almost to capacity and they have transformed Melbourne's theatre habits.

Of course, Melbourne is passionate about sport. I have always believed that kilo for kilo, muscle for muscle, Melburnians are more deeply devoted to sport of all kinds, than any creatures on earth. The biggest crowds for Australian Rules football, cricket, tennis, soccer, racing are generated in Melbourne. You might even say they are beserk, besotted, around the bend about football. There are no class lines in this. The late Professor Ian Turner of Monash University used to say that Melbourne was the one city where you could go to the university staff lavatory or the lavatory at the local pub and still hear the same conversation. It is even

Cutting swathes through the urban landscape, freeways attempt to resolve Melbourne's peak-hour traffic snarls and facilitate cross-city travel.

Above: *Eastern Freeway, east towards Doncaster.*

Below: *The complex patterns of the freeway interchange at St Kilda Junction.*

Above: *Bridge across the Maribyrnong, north-west of the city.*

Below: *The West Gate Bridge, crossing the lower Yarra.*

Intercolonial cricket was first played in Melbourne in 1856. It remains one of the city's most popular sports, whether at friendly club, or serious Test match level.

Pages 86–87: *St Vincent Gardens, Albert Park.*

politically dangerous for a premier or opposition leader not to show his allegiance to a footy team.

Football is discussed, worried about all the year round and attracts more than twice the spectators won by Rugby League in Sydney. I think there are three reasons for the Victorian obeisance to football. First, one has to admit — however reluctantly — that Australian Rules is the most spectacular and exciting of all codes of football.

Second, Melbourne was always a very tidy city, neatly laid out with wide symmetrical streets. It was never split in half by water like Sydney, and very early it had a superb public transport system: good suburban trains and the most comprehensive cable-tram system in the world. There were large self-contained suburbs all around the central city. What's more, they all disliked each other and were intensely competitive. The citizens of Richmond did not like the denizens of Fitzroy; the inhabitants of Essendon felt superior to those of South Melbourne; Collingwood detested the toffs of the Melbourne Football Club; and I think almost everybody loathed North Melbourne. So the game became very incestuous. The locals loved their club competition; they weren't even slightly concerned at what went on in Brisbane, Sydney, Adelaide and Perth. Interstate matches were, and still are, considered as tiresome interruptions to the weekly suburban war.

Third, Melbourne always had very superior sporting grounds. Even when Mr Stephenson's XI played at the Melbourne Cricket Ground on New Year's Day, 1862, it was considered the best-equipped cricket ground in the world. That situation has never altered. It is best to see the MCG when the stands are full. A yacht makes no show unless it has a full spinnaker, a full spread of canvas. When the stands are full at the MCG it becomes alive. It is awesome to see it filled with over 100 000 spectators on the day of the Grand Final. It is fascinating to listen to the moods of the crowd: the 'ohs' and 'ahs' going up and down as if controlled by the stops of an organ, or sudden explosions of boos. This can be heard kilometres away. An umpire knows he is alive when he is receiving an expression of opinion from 100 000 throats. Even more awe-inspiring are the silences — the truly expectant, excited silence, for example, when Malcolm Marshall starts his long run to bowl to Kepler Wessels in a one-day cricket match.

But if Melburnians were peculiar about cricket and football, very early they were also peculiar about horseracing. Again there is a good reason for this. Not enough credit has ever been given to R C Bagot and that wonder of the world, the Flemington Racetrack. Bagot had a hand in designing the two most deeply revered Melbourne institutions: the MCG and Flemington. He was the first secretary of the Victoria Racing Club and he had the idea, unique for 1864, that racing should be for the working man. He built a bluestone stand for the cash customers which was, for heaven's sake, better than the timber affair which had been provided for the members. He even threw open the Flat for no charge. The official crowd figure for the Melbourne Cup of 1880 was 100 000. When you consider that the entire population at that time was only 282 000, then better than one in every three people were at the races that day.

We have all sorts of city institutions: we have Moomba, the great festival which takes place in March every year; we have Australia Day; we have the Grand Final; we have Anzac Day; but the remarkable day which seems to bring out the ethos of Melbourne remains Cup Day, on the first Tuesday in November. We were the first people anywhere to devote a public holiday entirely to a horse race. According to the Catholic writer, John Francis Hogan, we should not be surprised at this: many of 'our dusky brethren in less civilised lands' selected their gods from the animal kingdom; therefore we should not be surprised when Australians made a national festival of horse worship.

Well, what's Melbourne like to look at? You may not believe this, but I am a sucker for the old Yarra. Always it has suffered from bad public relations. There are a million gags about the river which flows upside down, but I believe it is the most beautiful river in the country. The ride along the bicycle path on the south side is enchanting. I go along that track every morning and look at the reflection of the city towers in the water. Clouds of seagulls spring out of my way; always there are two or three ducks scudding across the water, and just occasionally a long-legged ibis or a black swan.

The earliest settlers found the Yarra a source of fresh water and a suitable berth for their ships. By the late nineteenth century Melbourne's docks were the hub of Australia's colonial shipping. The docks are still there but today the Yarra also serves as a focus for sport and recreation, both active and passive.

Ah, but in the evening that's the time, the best show in town. All the rowers are out: the sculls, fours, eights, kayaks, surf-club boats, masses of muscle under tension. The coaches on their ancient bicycles are panting up and down the path, shouting through microphones which I swear nobody hears. Here you observe the form of the Melbourne Grammar, Scotch and Wesley crews, and one dreams back to the 1930s when the schoolboy Head of the River was a vast social event second only to the Melbourne Cup.

Autumn on the Yarra is best of all and I recommend that you wander across Princes Bridge, particularly on a Wednesday evening, for at that time the bellringers are practising at St Paul's Cathedral. The bells provide the noblest peal outside the British Isles. Of the two cathedrals I think I prefer St Patrick's. St Patrick's is made of bluestone, a beautiful, hard, local stone. Bluestone is now as trendy as all hell; it is the stone for garden walls — preferably with cast-iron inserts — in Toorak, Camberwell and Brighton. Back in the 1850s and 1880s it was anything but. This was the working man's stone, the material for cobbled roads, gutters, woolstores and gaols — grim and formidable. When the time came in the 1880s to build St Paul's Cathedral the Anglican canons decided against bluestone and went for the more fashionable 'prettier' sandstone which they imported at great expense from Sydney. St Paul's sandstone deteriorated to such an extent that restoration cost a million dollars, but the working man's bluestone in St Patrick's will be good for another thousand years.

Port Phillip Bay has its good angles. It is lovely along the

Melbourne's bayside beaches provide respite from summer heat. Kerford Road pier (above left) *juts into Port Phillip Bay, while* (above), *further along Beaconsfield Parade, the rectangular grid of bayside development gives way to Albert Park, with its lake, golf links* (left) *and sporting fields.*

Esplanade at Middle Park, Brighton and Beaumaris, but the bayside around Cheltenham, Mordialloc, Edithvale, Chelsea and Seaford is pure drear. You are not allowed to see the water because the greed of previous generations has built houses right down to the water's edge.

The city is blessed like few places on earth with gardens: the Domain, the Botanic Gardens, the Alexandra Gardens, the Carlton Gardens, the Treasury Gardens, the Fitzroy and Flagstaff Gardens. There is a tan on the grand circuit around the Botanic Gardens. This is the very spot where in the old days you would be seen riding your horse. Now it is for the joggers, and they are there from early dawn in their hundreds, at the lunch hour in their multi-hundreds and they are still there panting late at night. There are males and even more young females. If you are fond of watching other humans taking exercise it is very satisfying.

St Kilda Road until ten years ago was a great boulevard, the best in Melbourne. Not any more. Now it is lined with streamlined office buildings that remind one of the awful 'Love Boat' on television. What is the best now? Well, I would give nine out of ten to Spring Street: the fine old Treasury Building is a classic beauty; then there is the Princess Theatre, which was already there when Burke and Wills set off on their strange expedition. It has everything: the archangel Gabriel blowing his trumpet; it has cupolas, urns, Corinthian columns, cast-iron balconies, minarets and even a ghost.

The best street now would be Royal Parade. For some reason it has escaped destruction. It is everything St Kilda Road used to be: a parade of stately houses rich with cast-iron.

Collins Street? I have tried to avoid talking about our beloved Collins Street. The Occidental, the Oriental, Melbourne Mansions, Ogg's Pharmacy; all are gone and the Paris End is no more. At one end we have the twin fifty-storey towers of Collins Place and at the other sixty storeys of the Rialto. The Rialto is the newcomer, 'the tallest office building in Australia', we are told. Always we have had a simple passion to possess the tallest and the grandest.

Some of the charm of the old Collins Street still remains and the National Trust has fought some desperate battles. So much so that many of the old buildings are now facades, like stage sets for a Gilbert and Sullivan opera. The antiquity is only paper thin: No. 1 Collins Street is a facade, the building that once was the Alexandra Club is a facade and the Winfield building by the Rialto is really a shell.

Melbourne for years now has been looking for a landmark and we have even had a disastrously unsuccessful landmark competition. Sydney has its Harbour Bridge, Brisbane has its City Hall: what was the one item immediately recognisable in Melbourne? Where was Melbourne's soul?

Of course, it has been there all the time. The trams. They, of all things, tell the story of the solidity and immutable character of Melbourne. Except Glenelg, and the odd place that runs a tourist tram, every other city in Australia has scrapped them. They had a dark Churchillian hour in the sixties when they were despised by the automobile lovers, but now they have come into the sun and are utterly loved — so much so, that other cities come to us: we are one of the last repositories in the world for vintage trams and we have shipped them in numbers to Portland and San Francisco in the United States.

Melbourne has just held its 150th birthday celebration — from nothing to three million in 150 years. Part of the fun was to hold a great party for the whole town. We moved in a thousand trees, stopped the trams and cars, and put wall-to-wall grass all down Swanston Street. I suspect there is hope for a town that can do anything as absurd as that.

Above: *Beaconsfield Parade and the bayside development along Port Phillip Bay.*

Right: *Marine Parade skirts Port Phillip Bay as it sweeps south. The Palais Theatre and Luna Park are in the foreground, centre, with St Kilda Marina to the right.*

Below: *Williamstown.*

Port Phillip Bay was discovered and claimed for Britain by Acting Lieutenant John Murray in 1802. It was first surveyed in 1803 and its shores permanently settled in 1835. The entrance from Bass Strait is narrow, but the bay's 225 kilometres of shoreline provide plenty of space for recreation.

Unplanned residential and industrial development, combined with urban and shipping waste, have created major environmental problems for Port Phillip. Today the impact of a multi-million dollar rescue program is being felt as levels of pollution and erosion fall and the bay once again becomes a retreat for city dwellers.

NO BOATING

Brisbane
HUGH LUNN

BRISBANE, though it is my home town, is not a pretty city. Its roads are acned, its buildings weathered. It is disorganised, tatty and hot.

If you asked most Australians which would be the last capital city they would wish to live in, or visit, they would almost certainly say, quite probably loudly, 'Brisbane'.

For Brisbane isn't a lot of things. It isn't the biggest; it isn't the remotest; it isn't the oldest; it isn't even the smallest. In fact the general impression, even in Brisbane, is that it is a pretty nondescript sort of city.

Travel writers, it seems, merely pass through it on the way to somewhere else. The average Sydneyite or Melburnian, headed for the Great Barrier Reef, condemns Brisbane with civil leer as 'a big country town'. Sydney grapejuice buff Leo Schofield wrote that Brisbane people used less house paint per head than in any other capital. British satirist Jilly Cooper, en route to Sydney, couldn't quite place it in the world: 'In the scorching sunlight the influences seem to come from New Orleans, the Wild West, and (Colonial) India — all at the same time.' And American travel writer John Godwin, on his way to the Gold Coast, wrote simply that Brisbane was 'frankly blah'.

Pages 100–101: *The Brisbane River winds through the city, spanned here by the Victoria, Captain Cook and Story bridges.*

Victoria Bridge crosses from South Brisbane into Queen Street, a major city artery and hub of the central business district. Part of Queen Street has been closed to traffic, to create an attractive shopping mall.

And yet, while all these views exist for a reason, they exist merely because these people only pass through. For while Sydney can be appreciated as you come in to land, and Adelaide looks lovely from the taxi window, you have to actually know Brisbane to enjoy it. Sure it looks neglected. There is absolutely no doubt its city buildings are a tangle of stylistic oddments left over from various eras and cultures: the French Renaissance Parliament House dwarfed by its concrete-and-glass annexe; the National Hotel's iron lacework verandahs near St John's Cathedral — stone Gothic on three sides with a fibro front (the money has not been found to complete it); an Italian Renaissance palazzo Treasury building; the old Museum building with silver-domed red-brick turrets reminiscent of Turkey; and fat blue or brown towers which look down on what was once the tallest building in town — the neo-classical City Hall, fronted by palm trees, with its giant dome and elegant clock tower.

In fact, the centre of Brisbane looks as if a bunch of European and North American architects from different centuries were thrown together to exhibit their work in a strange subtropical setting. Once you accept this, it makes inner Brisbane an interesting place to wander around. The view from the glass-sided elevator in the Sheraton — looking across the modern circle pattern of Anzac Square and Post Office Square to the vertical columns of the GPO — convinces you that the jumble sale that is Brisbane city can look beautiful when space is allowed between the buildings.

But even so, and no matter how many big buildings are looked at, a visitor would miss the real beauty of Brisbane — a beauty born to blush unseen and waste its sweetness on the locals. You won't see it driving down to the Gold Coast or north to the Barrier Reef or on the ugly drive in from the airport. The unique thing about Brisbane, and the reason I live here, is its old inner suburbs of large gardens dotted with verandahed timber homes — corrugated iron roofs (usually sun-faded dull red) above, and high wooden stumps below. These homes and their gardens provide a lifestyle that cannot be emulated elsewhere. Having lived in London, Singapore and Hong Kong, having seen Peking, Russia and Monte Carlo, and having survived a couple of years in Jakarta and Saigon, I have some idea of when I'm well off.

I purchased my home in 1977 for $51 000. It is not the classic timber colonial with wide verandahs on three sides and bay windows but a simpler version known locally as 'the Queenslander'. This style — with scores of variations on the theme — proliferates through the older suburbs. It has a wide front verandah shaded by wooden blinds, the ceilings are very high (for coolness) and the walls are of vertical pine VJ boards which fit one into the other. The lounge and dining room are inevitably divided by a high decorative timber arch and the floors are wide polished pine boards. Double doors, called 'French doors', open on to the verandah to let plenty of breeze through and the house is usually on stumps, most of which are more than two metres high.

It is these stumps which, probably more than anything else, cause disparaging remarks to be made about Brisbane. Yet they are the best feature of the house. People still argue in Brisbane about why the early settlers put their homes up on these stilts, as southerners call them. Some say it was because of fear of flooding; and if you have seen it rain in Brisbane you will understand that. Brisbane once recorded nearly a metre of rain in one day.

Flooding probably had something to do with it and there is also some truth in the theory that it was to 'get away from the snakes'. But I don't believe the Sydney journalist who wrote it was because Queenslanders believed mosquitoes couldn't fly higher than two metres — not from the way the mosquitoes like to gather on my white ceilings. Others say the stumps were to keep the timber homes away from the white ants which can very quickly eat out a timber house from inside the wood while you are unaware of their presence. The evidence for this theory is that the stumps of these homes invariably have a tin hat 'to stop the white ants reaching the timber'. But this theory would not account for some of the homes which, in the hillier suburbs like Paddington, have stumps up to eight metres long. It is these hilly homes that provide the clue to the real reason for Brisbane's stumps.

Because old Brisbane was built across a series of hills and gullies there are very few flat pieces of land: this is what one would expect in a city built in a heavy rainfall area above a big river. Without bulldozers to level the land, the cheapest method of building a

From above, Brisbane's bridges, freeways and expressways form complex patterns of lines, swirls, curves and arches. The city's location on both sides of the river has caused considerable traffic problems which are only now being attacked in a systematic way.

Jet
Ansett.

level home was to put it on stumps. The unexpected bonus of doing this is that in the middle of summer the area under the house is very cool, not just because the rooms above provide a layer of insulation but because the method of enclosing the area beneath — vertical wood battens nailed a few centimetres apart — allows the breeze through.

The height of the homes, though it provides better views, probably also explains why so few Brisbane homes have the high fences that find such favour in Melbourne. A two-metre wooden fence doesn't provide any extra privacy if your house is sitting up above it. Thus, few Brisbane people build fences, and this produces an annoying by-product: sometimes the old Brisbane suburbs appear to be populated mainly by dogs roaming in groups. And, because Brisbane has never really had a serious security problem, those with fences usually leave the gate open. The dog problem has been ignored by a City Council which, unlike any other Australian city, rules the entire city and is therefore unable and unwilling to take notice of purely local problems. An unfortunate result of the lack of local councils is that there is no appeal to local loyalties. In fact, the city's largely tatty appearance can no doubt be blamed on its monolithic government.

'The jumble sale that is Brisbane city can look beautiful when space is allowed between the buildings.' The neo-classical City Hall (below left) *is dwarfed by modern commercial towers, while* (below and right) *Anzac Square and the Central Railway buildings are similarly overwhelmed by the tall buildings of modern finance, commerce and government.*

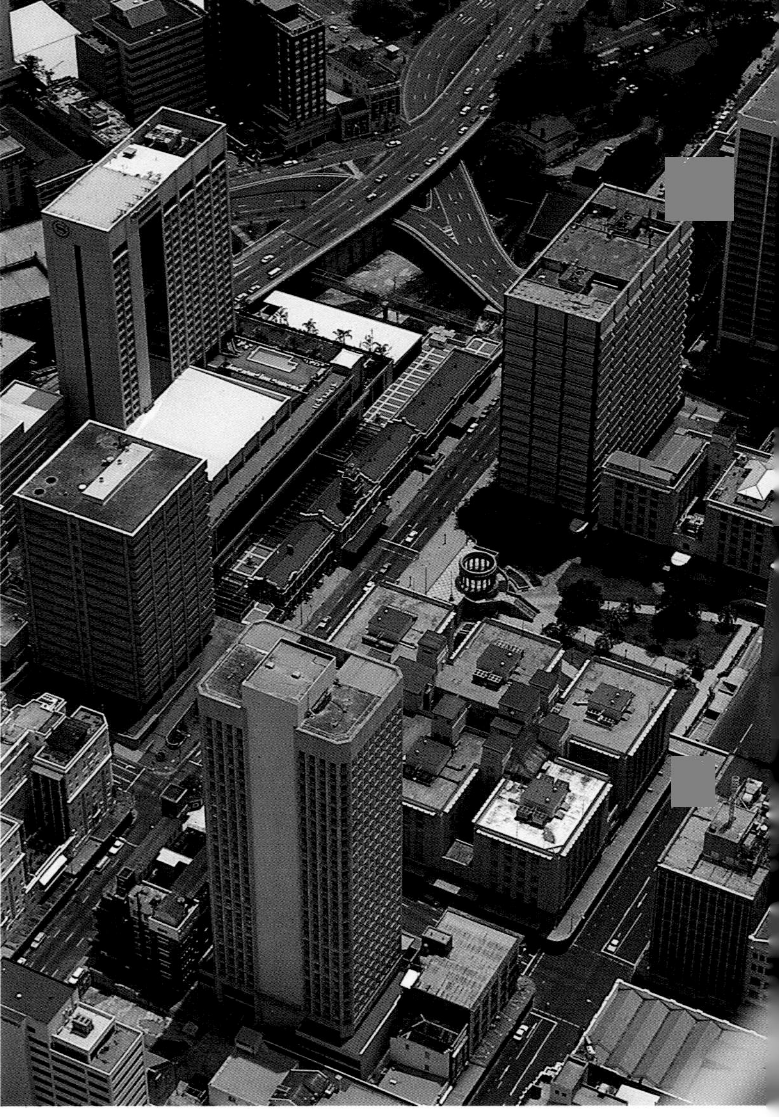

A city of changing light and mood: the city centre looking south (above); *City Hall glowing at dusk* (above left); *and a city parking station towards the end of day* (right).

Perhaps it also explains the worst aspect of the Brisbane garden: the incinerator down in the corner as far from the owner's house and, therefore, as close to the neighbour's, as possible. In an evening ritual which smokes out neighbours and pollutes the city, householders all over town burn most of their rubbish because, in a hot, humid city, the Brisbane City Council elects to collect the garbage only once a week — and then limits it to one bin which must not be heavy.

But, back inside his timber home, the Brisbanite can happily ignore those problems.

My second favourite thing about my Queenslander is its roof. That may seem a strange thing to say, because in all the cities I have lived in or visited the one thing you never think about or notice is your roof. But a corrugated iron roof is something you cannot ignore for long. It drums you to sleep when the heavy drops of summer rain beat down loudly and it wakes you up when a heavy mango, waxing over-mellow, drops on a silent summer night, or when the possums chase each other from roof to tree and back again. And the iron roof ensures that you never miss a hailstorm — which would be like missing the first snowfall in London. Three weeks ago the hail hit my roof so loudly and so often that the house became a giant speaker box beating out a dozen versions of the 1812 overture all at once, exciting all the senses while ice overflowed from the roof gutters and individual pieces bounced off the back landing and patio. And, when the storm was over — with terracotta tiles on modern houses smashed to pieces — my corrugated iron roof was dinted, but unbowed.

These gigantic summer storms of course mean that trees grow really well in Brisbane gardens. There are few timber homes with-

out at least one mango tree, plus a couple of pawpaw trees, near the back stairs so that it is easy to pick the fruit fresh from the back landing.

I have two Bowen mango trees, a large stand of ladyfinger banana trees, a passionfruit vine, a loquat tree, and two Queensland nut trees. Actually you really need a Queensland home to enjoy Queensland nuts. They are round, brown and very, very hard and the only way to get at the nut is to find a crack in the concrete under the house, insert the nut, and hit it with a steel hammer. The difficult art is to hit it only hard enough to crack the shell and not the nut. If you don't put it in a concrete crack the nut will fly off into the air in any direction like ricocheting shrapnel.

But the real reason I have so many trees is not so much for their produce as for their shade and beauty: they add a new dimension to the garden and attract lots of birds. For it would be a pity to live in Brisbane and not take advantage of being able to grow a stand of palms, or a giant scented camphor laurel, or to create the spreading crowns of red or lilac of the poinciana or the jacaranda. I have two red-flowered coral trees and two pink-flowered parrot trees, both of which bring the parrots: some green, some blue and deep scarlet. The blue and yellow ones come just for the grass

seeds. The branches of my trees spread almost into my verandah because of its height, so I get a close view of the birds and sometimes the smell of the flowers permeates right through the house — especially the honey smell from the torelliana eucalypts and the night-scented jasmine.

But there are disadvantages too in being able to get so close to nature. I haven't seen any snakes, but large garden spiders — and I hate spiders — are common in the house. When venturing from the house at night I carry a stick to clear cobwebs and a torch to make sure I don't trip over a big ugly cane toad on my way to the tennis shed for a barbecue. And, while the fruit and blossoms attract the parrots by day, by night they bring down the giant bats which fly over Brisbane on summer nights, literally in their hundreds of thousands. It is scary to disturb them: they are as big as cats with wings, and they take off unexpectedly with a big flap of black.

The trees also harbour mosquitoes and each summer evening you must spray your ankles unless your house is screened; but screens cut down on breezes and spoil the look of the old Queenslander built in hardier times. Some people report problems with the scrub turkeys which they say peck holes in their milk-bottle tops. But the only problem I have encountered with birds was when two swamp pheasants — large, beautiful tail-feathered

Left: *The French Renaissance-style Parliament House, opened in 1868, is dwarfed by its modern concrete and glass annexe.*

Below: *Relaxing on a hotel rooftop.*

Pages 112–113: *The Brisbane River is the largest commercial river in Australia. On the right is the cantilevered Story Bridge, completed in 1940.*

AMP
CityMutual
CITICORP
NATIONAL BANK

CityMutual
ANZ
NATIONAL BANK

creatures — fought it out on the tennis court while I was waiting to play.

There is an abundance of trees in Brisbane and it is not unusual in many of the older suburbs to see a frill-necked lizard where gardens meet or to have a frightening encounter with a blue-tongue lizard — his bright blue tongue touching off scare signals in the brain.

The source of this teeming wildlife is never far away in Brisbane. It is the giant winding river, fed by a thousand tiny streams from the high wooded hills to the west that dominate the city and its sunsets. Wherever you are in Brisbane these ranges are in full view. They come to within several kilometres of the city centre itself and stretch to distant peaks like Mt Glorious from where the city seems a mere ripple on the landscape. If you go up to Mt Coot-tha in Brisbane, or Mt Nebo or Mt Glorious, you will see sights unmatched elsewhere in Australia and, I suspect, the world.

It is because of these hills that the Brisbane River is crossed by the magnificent Story Bridge — the largest bridge designed and built by Australians. (In Australia it is second in size only to the Sydney Harbour Bridge which was designed in London with the steel parts made in Yorkshire.) The Story Bridge was designed by a Brisbane engineer, Dr John Job Crew Bradfield, who wrote that he built such a complex cobweb of steel because: 'The tree clad

Left: *The city centre looking towards South Brisbane. The Botanic Gardens can be seen on the left. Established in 1865 and now covering 20 hectares, the gardens are on the site of the settlement's first fruit and vegetable garden.*

Below: *Customs House at Petrie Bight, completed in 1889.*

The AMP building is among the more spectacular of Brisbane's modern edifices. Renewed urban development is indicative of Brisbane's progress.

hills encircling the city indicated that the cantilever type of bridge, with its lofty towers and powerful river arms, would best harmonize with the picturesque and rugged beauty of the Brisbane skyline. A cantilever bridge, with its plated angles, its bold towers and broad shoulders — whether viewed nearby or afar off — will express simplicity, strength, and grace'.

Bridges are a feature of Brisbane because of the need to traverse such a wide and fearful flooding river which has washed away a couple of big bridges in its time. At Indooroopilly there is a bridge with homes built into the towers where families have lived for decades. Near the city there is a bridge of concrete arches and, in recent times, a very high suspended box-girder bridge — the Gateway — has been built to allow large ships to pass underneath. But, because the river divides the entire city, Brisbane's six road and two railway bridges are still not sufficient.

The river is such a barrier that the garbage contractors, the dog catchers and even plumbers stick to either the south or the north side. Even many tennis teams play only northside or southside competitions. Yet few more bridges are likely to be built because no northside or southside suburb wants a bridge bringing heavy traffic through its streets.

You would think that the lack of bridges would bring about a boom in cross-river ferries but, despite the pleasures of this form of travel, ferry services have actually declined over the years. In fact the Brisbane River is so little used that newspapers periodically conduct campaigns with the theme, 'Let's use our river'. But,

The new Queensland Cultural Centre, South Brisbane (extreme right, above) *contains the state's art collection, a museum and library, an auditorium and performing arts centre.*

perhaps because access to the river is limited almost exclusively to the homes that front it, there has been little response.

The first prominent Brisbane person to recognise the river's potential was architect Robin Gibson who built Brisbane's magnificent outward-looking Cultural Centre on the banks of the unfashionable southside, with an internal canal paralleling the river and a huge fountain in the river itself.

But maybe the real answer is first to clean up the river. Oldies say that when they were children it was blue. Once people sunbaked on the sand underneath the Indooroopilly Bridge and swam in the river. But now it is dredged for gravel and polluted by industry and the populace — and even by the City Council every time it has a sewerage breakdown. Now it is murky brown and one feels that the best way for Brisbane to start improving its image would be to look first at its river.

It is all the more important since the river leads into Moreton Bay on the city's eastern shores. This exotic bay should be as big a talking point among Australians as is Sydney Harbour, but it is little known. It is like an inland ocean splashed liberally with islands, very large and very small. Parts of it take more than half an hour to cross in a speedboat. The bay is full of fish — as well as large sharks — and some of the island beaches within 15 kilometres of the city suburbs have beaches as good as most on the Barrier Reef (like Horseshoe Bay on Peel Island).

Right: *An outdoor performance in King George Square in front of the City Hall.*

Below: *Nudgee College, Boondall.*

Ansett

Storm clouds over the city. Most of Brisbane's annual rainfall of 1090 millimetres falls between December and March and the summer storms can be torrential and spectacular.

The city by night. Parliament House and its annexe (above); *and* (right) *the Italian Renaissance Treasury Building with the Executive Building and government offices behind it.*

Hayles

The surprise is that, like the river, the bay is so little used — probably because the Gold and Sunshine Coasts are only an hour from the city. But that has been part of the change in modern Brisbane. Once Brisbane people swam in the river or in the bay at Wynnum or caught a boat down the river to Redcliffe. But in the last 20 years much of that has changed. As the city has expanded out into nearby shires — Albert, Logan, Pine Rivers, Moreton — the new arrivals and the young have, like the architects in the city centre, opted for imported house styles. The outer suburbs are now crowded with haciendas, Roman villas and clay pillboxes. The delicate, unimposing timber architecture of the old Queenslanders has been replaced by the imposing, though inappropriate, strength and grandness of brick arches and concrete columns. The old landscape was determined by hill slope, trees and tracks but these modern suburbs repeat the grid pattern of Sydney, Melbourne and anywhere else with their wettex lawns and with the only vertical objects being pencil pines or Hills Hoists.

For a long time there the Queensland home went out of fashion, even with the locals; but luckily people are now flocking back as they realise the disadvantages of the clay hut from the south. The only trouble is that the council bureaucracy has allowed some modern monstrosities to be built in the old landscape and every now and then an entire block of timber and iron homes is spoilt by one brick one with a Roman-columned verandah and two sliding aluminium garage doors under brick arches as its main features. In the heartland of Brisbane's most beautiful old Queenslanders one developer built his contribution to Brisbane lifestyle: three houses in a row — a Sydney terrace, a Swiss chalet and a Cape Cod. That is something Brisbane is going to have to live with when, like Australia itself, it one day finally establishes the identity it has had all the time.

Meanwhile, the restaurants which have filled all the old corner stores and butcher shops have been a plus, providing lots of local eating places in a familiar landscape. And there are even a couple of builders in Brisbane who now specialise solely in building old Queensland homes — and they are in great demand.

Brisbane might not be pretty, but it is unique: from the cries of the curlews at night to the bats hanging electrocuted from the overhead wires; from the mass exodus every January to beat the heat to roads down hillsides which are so steep that a Scandinavian roadbuilding engineer screamed with terror as I turned into Miskin Street, Toowong — he thought we had gone over a cliff.

And I'm not the only person to notice.

French travel writer Pierre Grundmann: 'Brisbane is the greenest city of Australia — tropical green . . . green of palm trees, bougainvilleas and frangipani trees . . . meat, fish (including shell fish), its tropical fruits (pawpaws, mangoes and avocado pears), and its gardens are top quality. Brisbane's cuisine well reflects the influence of all these products.'

Right: *Brisbane's City Hall, completed in 1930, occupies a site of almost a hectare. An imposing building of Queensland freestone, it is surmounted by a huge dome and clock tower over ninety metres high. Between the City Hall and the nearby State Government Insurance Office (SGIO) is the Albert Street Uniting Church* (below).

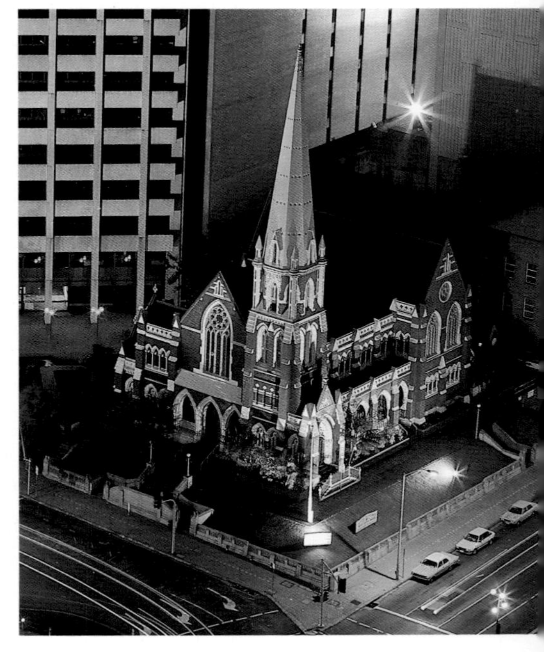

ONLY
TAXIS
AND
BUS

Jet
Ansett.

Brisbane jazz player and journalist David Bentley: 'I hope Brisbane never turns into the sort of twee, precious, upward mobile coterie of brass doorknocker polishers and sandstone chippers of the sort gathered in smug self-congratulation around Sydney's Balmain and Paddington. Brisbane fits like an old shoe. Some parts of it may even resemble an old shoe. But, if we're scruffy, we do it with a certain style.'

And, finally, Jilly Cooper again: 'Brisbane at dusk was magical. The huge river turned to mother-of-pearl under its Meccano bridge, a lemon yellow sunset gilded the grey-green acacias and softened the rose pink roofs and the trellis of pylons along the hills.'

Left: *Looking upriver. The William Jolly Bridge in the centre was named to honour the city's first mayor. Beyond is a new railway bridge.*

Below: *Part of the Queen Street Mall.*

Looking towards the city from South Brisbane. The five-spanned Captain Cook Bridge on the right was completed in 1972. Beyond it are the illuminated cliffs of the Brisbane River on the Botanic Gardens reach (right).

Conias Apollo
REAL ESTATE
444048

Adelaide
CHRIS MILNE

Pages 132–133: *Adelaide, a city of parklands and open spaces. A view from the north with the River Torrens separating the city centre from North Adelaide. The Adelaide Children's Hospital is in the centre.*

The ordered greenery of North Adelaide's public golf course gives way to Adelaide Oval, with the city centre across the Torrens.

ADELAIDE, named for an English queen and affecting a regal air, nestles neatly between sea and hills on the edge of farmland. On a hot summer's day the arced, purple and brown backdrop of the Mount Lofty Ranges shimmers in the heat haze; the trees along North Terrace, the city's handsome equivalent of a Parisian boulevard, droop and the birds shelter songless in the branches. Down on the bank of the placid River Torrens, the sun glares off the Festival Centre's segmented white roof and highlights the ornate Victorian rotunda on the deserted lawns. It's a scorcher, people agree, and the radio announcers, reverting to Fahrenheit, talk about the temperature 'topping the century mark'. People seek out the shady side of streets, the shadows of colonial and cantilever verandahs, the cool courtyards where fountains play. The pace of life, never rapid, becomes sluggish.

Adelaide, still an agricultural centre despite the growth of manufacturing industry since World War II, is reputedly a staid, solid and comfortable provincial city, moving to the calm rhythm of the seasons, the slow ripening of the grapes on the vines which still cling to the suburban fringes. The city's encircling parklands, with paddocks where horses still run free and where, until a couple of decades ago, small dairy herds were kept behind gates marked 'Cows Only', add to the rural ambience.

'A great place to bring up children', is the most-repeated phrase from locally born residents and refugees from the more frenetic and crowded cities of the east. Yet that is only one facet of a city that was founded on radical principles and that has championed political and social reform — from female suffrage to the legalising of homosexual behaviour; from consumer protection to Aboriginal land rights — and fostered technological innovation from the stump jump plough to the iron lung, to the intricate electronic fault-finding heart of the RAAF's FA 18 fighters. While operating some of the country's oldest trams — delightful timber-panelled vehicles which rock their way between the city centre and the coast at Glenelg — Adelaide is building Australia's most advanced transport system: the O-Bahn guided bus which will speed commuters at 100 kilometres an hour down its concrete busway through the River Torrens valley.

Adelaide is as complex and complicated as any modern city. It is also 'different' in its own ways. That difference, and the city's character, are hard to define.

Various writers and visitors have grappled with the problem. Australian writer Douglas Aiton found Adelaide 'the most progressive, pleasing and elegant city in Australia . . . it has preserved a lifestyle resurrecting some of the dignity and grace of an earlier age'.

The British columnist Bernard Levin, after a visit to the Adelaide Festival of Arts, said the city had retained 'the placid grandeur of the era of certainty'. He added: 'This beautiful ciy is so immaculately groomed that it seems to have been slightly enbalmed.'

The US magazine *Gourmet* enthused: 'Some childhood fantasies not only live up to but exceed reality; Adelaide fits that category . . . it remains the most gracious city Down Under . . . green parklands and the bluestone houses create an atmosphere unique not just in Australia but in the world.'

But Salman Rushdie, a Booker Prize winner writing in Britain's *Tatler* magazine, had a different perspective. He read reports of murder and arson in the newspapers, experienced disorientation and decided it was an ideal setting for a horror movie: 'Adelaide is Amityville, or Salem, and things here go bump in the night.'

Adelaide was founded in 1836 after a bitter dispute over its site by the first settlers. Kingscote on Kangaroo Island, Port Lincoln at the entrance to Spencer Gulf, and Encounter Bay near the mouth of the River Murray were the preferred sites of different groups. Colonel William Light, an English officer-surveyor, who had been sent to South Australia by the Colonisation Commissioners in London to select a suitable site, clashed with the first governor, John Hindmarsh, but claimed good geographical reasons — including

Right: *Colonel Light's plan of 1837 provided for a city centre surrounded by parklands. Despite rapid suburban growth, the parkland has remained as a green belt around the city. A view of the South Parklands, with Glen Osmond Road leading into the city.*

Below: *Adelaide International Airport.*

Above: *The Anglican Cathedral of St Peter, North Adelaide, dates from 1878. Behind, fringing the Torrens, is the symbolic Cross of Sacrifice.*

Right: *The Torrens, named for the chairman of the South Australian Colonisation Commissioners, runs through Adelaide from east to west. Immediately behind are buildings of the University of Adelaide.*

permanent water, a good anchorage and potential port, and access to the hinterland — for his choice of site on the sheltered eastern shore of St Vincent Gulf.

He placed Adelaide on the edge of a large creek, which was named the River Torrens, beneath a sweep of hills with a hump called Mt Lofty. The nomenclature reflected the bounding optimism of the founders, who came ashore and camped by the billabongs at Holdfast Bay, while they planned and built the capital of the new colony a dozen kilometres inland. William Light drew up a grid plan for the city, with a stepped eastern boundary above the bank of a gum-lined creek, and five squares to break up the pattern of the wide streets. Across the river, on the high bank, he planned a residential section to a quite different pattern, with another central square. Around the two areas, and through the river valley between, he designated a great swathe of parklands.

The people to fill this planned city came mostly from England, attracted by an innovative colonisation scheme devised by Edward Gibbon Wakefield while he was in London's Newgate Prison. He had been imprisoned there for three years for abducting a young heiress, whom he had married at Gretna Green without the permission of her furious parents.

His 1829 scheme for 'scientific' settlement was finally accepted by the Colonial Office in 1834. It sought to establish a colony free from the land grabbing and squatting of eastern Australia, and proposed that the controlled and systematic sale of land would finance the emigration of the skilled and unskilled workers to meet the needs of the expanding colony. There would be no convicts. Apart from a few convict runaways from the east, who had set themselves up in tiny isolated communities as hunters and sealers, Wakefield was the new colony's only link with penal servitude — an important social and commercial factor in its future development. Wakefield envisaged an ordered model colony which would have, in the words of local historian Derek Whitelock, a 'well regulated gentry and free and honest yeomen'.

South Australia was founded by capitalist entrepreneurs, some already wealthy, some seeking to found their fortunes. They wanted the colony to pay its own way and not rely on British government support. In fact, the experiment failed. The high hopes of funding the colony's growth through controlled land sales were dashed by speculators, and the quasi-independent colony effectively reverted to the Crown within five years, with the Colonial Office making a large grant to bail it out of financial trouble. But the opening up of good farming land, and then the discovery of copper in the early 1840s, rescued the colony from impending bankruptcy. Its business leaders, after initial squabbles, settled down to the business of making their investments pay. They financed expeditions in search of new farming and grazing lands in the uncompromising bush while recreating a slice of Olde England on the banks of the River Torrens, which they envisaged as an Antipodean River Thames and later dammed to provide a deeper and

Above: *St Peter's College, alma mater of much of Adelaide's 'establishment'.*

Right: *The rose garden, conservatory and artificial lake of the Botanic Gardens.*

Far right: *Aligned in death as in battle, servicemen lie buried in the AIF section of the cemetery in the West Parklands.*

wider stream on which to run Henley-on-Torrens rowing regattas.

The new society on the shores of St Vincent Gulf came with a ready-made reflection of English society in the 1830s. It was arguably the most 'English' of the Australian colonies and, despite the dramatic changes in social structure wrought by postwar immigration from mainland Europe, genteel Adelaide retains a strong social stratification, an elitism, a flavour of landed gentry. The Establishment of the Old Adelaide Families, derided as OAFS by their detractors, continues to dominate important areas. Many of their pioneering ancestors made their fortunes in the land speculation which almost wrecked the new colony and its proposed orderly settlement, and in agricultural and pastoral pursuits. They took up huge tracts of the state, and some retain large holdings still, exerting a strong influence through agriculture on Adelaide's commercial life. They control key business sectors. Their favourite school, St Peter's College, turns out a disproportionate number of future leaders in business, the professions and politics. At the beginning of the 1980s, the Liberal premier, the Labor opposition leader and the parliamentary leader of the Australian Democrats were all old scholars of the school.

The elite inhabit the elegant mansions of North Adelaide and Medindie, the 'gentrified' former workmen's cottages in the eastern section of the city, the cooler foothill suburbs of Burnside and Kensington Gardens, and the secluded, wooded Adelaide Hills

By day and night, Victoria Square is the focal point of the city. The fountain, designed by John Dowie, is aligned with the major thoroughfare of King William Street. Around it, in surprising harmony, stand ornate Victorian buildings such as the Town Hall and General Post Office and modern towers like the Hilton International.

HILTON

The essence of Adelaide: Adelaide Oval (above), *looking south to the Festival Arts Centre and city; Government House* (left); *the Arts Centre, opened in 1973* (above right); *and Parliament House, the Arts Centre, King William Street and the old railway station* (right).

NICHOLAS NICKLEBY

towns and farmlets behind Mt Lofty. They patronise the arts, and founded the biennial Adelaide Festival of Arts, which is Australia's most concentrated and often most exciting arts event. Their ancestral home is the Adelaide Club, a solid stone building with iron railings and a big brass doorbell on North Terrace, across the road from Government House and a hundred metres or so from Parliament House. It excludes women from the padded leather sanctuary of its main clubrooms; they have to enter from a lane to reach the upstairs reception and dining rooms.

Elitism may be one of the least attractive aspects of Adelaide life, but for many residents it is only dimly acknowledged, if at all. Modern materialism, as rampant here as anywhere in Australia, has helped to found new fortunes; new technocrats have ascended to positions of power and influence. Nevertheless, despite its myopic drawbacks, elitism has helped to instill a striving for excellence, a feeling of quiet confidence, a sense of style and an appreciation of quality, which are cultural characteristics of Adelaide.

The concept of the colony was decidedly different from previous models particularly the penal settlement model of New South Wales and Tasmania. The new South Australian settlers were mostly independently minded pioneers, prepared to undertake an experiment in free settlement within the commercial charter of the South Australian Company. They came free of the prejudices which

Pages 146–151: *At dusk and by night, the city lights stretch over the plain on which Adelaide is built. Only the relatively small cluster of buildings in the commercial and business sector of the city are highlighted against the flat expanse of suburbia.*

IMFC

surrounded the penal settlements, too. Religious equality was guaranteed, and the colony welcomed other free-thinkers. Consequently, South Australia became a haven for some of Europe's harassed religious groups — Quakers, German Lutherans, Irish Catholics — and it became, in time, the 'city of churches'. Scattered through the city still are cathedrals, churches and chapels of a dozen different denominations, and an old Moslem mosque, built by the Afghan camel drivers who opened up the outback by providing the first transport system.

The leaders of early Adelaide combined their restraint and respectability from the outset with a spirit of radicalism. This was the 'paradise of dissent', and the dissenting traditions remain, although they have been eclipsed from time to time by another trait: wowserism. Although, in the early 1850s, South Australia was the first British colony to break the bond between church and state, some influences remained strong, particularly those of the industrious but sober Methodists. Some of the earliest colonists railed against excesses, particularly drink which, once the first grape vines were planted along the River Torrens, became plentiful. A century later, through the 1950s and into the early 1960s, Adelaide's killjoy image was well established; it was the city that died at 6 p.m. when the pubs, and almost everything else, closed. Yet that was an aberration which was swept away in the reforming and permissive 1970s, when Adelaide reverted to its former liveliness.

With the modern decline of religion, at least two former city churches have become restaurants. Indeed, food is something of a religion in this city, which is as well endowed with restaurants to serve its residents as any other in the country. With three major wine districts nearby, a coastline with abundant seafood, and orchards and market gardens on its outskirts, the ingredients are bountiful; and the Mediterranean climate encourages a Mediterranean approach to the pleasures of life.

But it is time for a closer look at the fabric of the city. The first buildings were made from mud and wattle but, with a lack of good building timber on the plains and a wish to establish an air of permanency, the settlers quarried the local stone and left Adelaide with a legacy of fine, solidly made buildings.

Behind the English ash and plane trees of North Terrace stand the public buildings, State Library, Museum, Art Gallery and University (which a century ago was one of the first in the world to admit women to its faculties). Along the main thoroughfare of King William Street, with its central plantation of lawns and flowers, are the banks; and radiating to left and right are the pastoral houses and commercial headquarters. Hidden behind the office blocks of the central district is the decorative Stock Exchange, one of the very few places in casually dressed Adelaide where suits are still worn.

Also radiating from the northern end of King William Street is bustling Rundle Mall, with its concentration of department and

Some Adelaide buildings: Islamic mosque (below); *Greek Orthodox church* (above left); *Carclew Youth Performing Arts Centre* (above right); *Lutheran seminary* (centre left); *Glenside Hospital* (centre right); *and Woodlands Girls Grammar School* (below right).

speciality shops, outdoor and balcony cafes. Buskers work their pitches, watched by shoppers and knots of noisily self-conscious young people who use the mall as a meeting place. Networks of shopping arcades riddle the buildings on both sides. Opposite Rundle Mall is Hindley Street, the entertainment centre. It is full of cinemas, amusement arcades, pubs, nightclubs, strip joints, sex shops and restaurants.

Around Victoria Square, William Light's pivot, are some delightful colonial relics: the white Treasury building, the sandstone Government offices, the bluestone Supreme Court, the handsome GPO and, just around the corner in King William Street, the balconied Town Hall where municipal government was founded in 1840 — the first in the British Empire and a tribute to the democratic principles on which the first settlers insisted. But Victoria Square — sadly fragmented by roadways now, terminus for the city's last remaining tram service and, in one section, a 'tribal ground' for Aborigines who meet and drink there — is also host to modern buildings which tower above the historic ones. One, the Reserve Bank, has character; others are graceless monoliths. But the colonial facade of the old Marine and Harbours building was rolled sideways in an exacting engineering feat to preserve it, and the new court buildings beside the Hilton Hotel were fashioned inside the shell of a grand old department store which, in 1948, provided the city with its most spectacular fire.

Preserving the past has become an industry in Adelaide. Old buildings and pubs, which in Sydney would fall to the demolition hammer, are often preserved in Adelaide. Developers are encouraged to renovate, or at least retain, the facade of 'character' buildings, and the city has its own planning commission and heritage

The Adelaide Hills, at the foothills of the Mount Lofty Ranges east of the city, have long been a retreat for those who appreciated the peace of rural living within easy reach of the metropolis. Some of their serenity is now being threatened as suburban development edges further into the hills.

The waters of St Vincent Gulf provide recreation for Adelaideans. Popular resorts are Semaphore (above) *and the Football Park at West Lakes* (left). *At Glenelg* (right and over), *Captain Hindmarsh in 1836 proclaimed the colony of South Australia and was sworn in as its first governor. Today this prominent beachside resort is linked to Adelaide by the state's only surviving tramline. The Patawalonga boat haven provides moorings and a system of locks for entry and exit into the Gulf.*

NEW WORLD & VARIETY STORE
Action FOOD BARN

list. When a building is threatened, groups quickly appear with banners and petitions to try to save it. They have scored some notable successes. When an ornate colonial bank building, an architectural treasure, faced demolition, a citizens' movement created such a storm that the developers were forced to abandon their plans. The state government refurbished the building and it became the Registry Office; its high-vaulted banking chamber is used for chamber music concerts and poetry readings. The state government was applauded for saving an historic North Terrace mansion which has been converted to an elegant restaurant (with a bistro in its stables) and whose grand rooms are used for state receptions.

Adelaide's Central Market, a colourful conglomeration of stalls selling fruit, vegetables, plants and smallgoods, has been saved from sterile supermarket-style redevelopment by another long campaign. Its unpretentious, slightly shabby character makes it attractive to many Adelaideans who come to haggle cheerfully with the stallholders on market days. Here, raucous Australian butchers, as well as Greek and Italian fruiterers, shout out their bargains. A much quieter influx in recent years of Indo-Chinese refugees who throng to the market, has resulted in the growth of Asian speciality food stores and little restaurants on the fringes.

Not all the conservation battles have been won. People bemoan the loss of the old South Australian Hotel, which is remembered with reverence as a classic colonial institution, with its sweeping staircase and its mannered ways. The British pop group, the Beatles, drew their biggest crowd when they appeared on its balcony, for Adelaide is always keen to embrace visiting celebrities. The old building made way for a modern edifice which commands splendid views but not much respect for its visual appeal. The Aurora, a curious city pub with German pioneer connections, was demolished during the night to foil pickets: and the Grange vineyards in the foothills, home of one of Australia's premier wines, was lost to subdivision after a monumental battle over its retention.

Nevertheless, Adelaide tends to protect its heritage with unusual intensity and pride. Living trends have helped, too. Old stone and brick cottages, terraces and houses within the city — some of them derelict — have been beautifully restored as the more affluent citizens move back to the inner areas. Adelaide City Council has fostered a return to city living with 'street-scaping' and tree planting to enhance the south-eastern corner of the city particularly. Corner shops have returned, restaurants and coffee houses opened; BMWs and Volvos have replaced the battered Holdens in the streets and little lanes as low-income families are pushed out of this former working-class enclave by the process of urban revitalisation and gentrification.

The south-west section is less fashionable. Here, in the rows of little cottages, low-income families retain a foothold although the pressure of rising property values and petrol prices, which

increase the attraction of inner-city dwellings, is mounting on them. However, the state's Housing Commission, once a broad-acre developer, is active in the inner city areas as well, so the city of Adelaide is destined to retain a healthy mix of population and ages.

Across the parklands to the south and east a similar process has occurred, and this is now spreading through the inner western suburbs as well. Postwar immigrants from southern Europe, attracted by the cheapness of property as well as its closeness to the city, have strongholds in the inner suburbs, but they are being joined by young professionals now. Norwood, to the east of the city, is perhaps the most homogeneous and cosmopolitan part of Adelaide, its shops and malls resounding to a gabble of tongues. Saturday morning shopping and coffee drinking on Norwood Parade is a prominent social event.

The only area to resist the change in character so far is the 'pughole country' in the shadow of an old gasometer in Brompton and Bowden. Here, clay laid down by the River Torrens was once excavated for brickmaking, and a suburb of little workers' cottages grew up around the job opportunities. Although Adelaide has avoided entangling itself in serpentine freeway systems, a plan for a land-consuming 'connector' freeway with a big interchange at Brompton cast a shadow over the twin suburbs, and urban blight worsened. The local residents, backed by activists, mounted a long campaign to save their area, and recently won the day — largely helped by the fact that traffic growth had not reached its predicted levels. The freeway plan was dropped, and now many cottages are being upgraded; those that have fallen into disrepair will be replaced with new Housing Commission cottages and flats, and the pugholes will become parks.

Compared to Sydneysiders and Melburnians, Adelaideans are more likely to drive to town to attend a theatrical performance or concert, to meet in a pub or eat at a restaurant, to participate in community activities. Community art is increasingly popular and one group won local council support to decorate the ubiquitous and ugly stobie poles that carry power lines through the suburbs. Adelaide has a way of honouring the arts, and the Adelaide Festival Centre, with its three performing arts venues and its outdoor amphitheatre, is the temple to the flourishing arts scene.

Adelaide is a sociable city, largely because of its convenience. No suburb is more than thirty minutes from the city centre, so it is simple to slip out to see friends. 'Everyone knows everyone in Adelaide' is a highly inaccurate although often-quoted cliche in a city of 950 000 people. But social circles do touch and overlap frequently and this helps to keep a rare conviviality and an intimacy alive. That, when it is all boiled down, is the innate charm of the place and its people: qualities that mark its difference as surely as its preserved colonial architecture, its spaciousness and unostentatious elegance.

Page 160–161: *Glenelg, with Jetty Road and the pier in the centre and Patawalonga boat haven to the right.*

Right and Below: *Swimming, fishing, playing or just lounging around along the shores of St Vincent Gulf. Matthew Flinders, who discovered the gulf in 1802, named it to honour the Earl of St Vincent; to the Aborigines it was Wongayerlo, 'western sea'.*

BP
CITY MUTUAL
PARMELIA HILTON
MLC
AMP AMP

Perth
HUGH SCHMITT

City Mutual
AMP AMP
GRIFFIN GRIFFIN

Pages 164–165: *The Narrows Interchange curves along the banks of the Swan River, with the city centre in the background.*

Views from the Swan River north to the city. The Barrack Street jetty (left) *leads through the Esplanade on the riverbank to the city centre. The large tower block* (below) *is Allendale Square, winner of the Royal Australian Institute of Architects' design award in 1978. To its left are the prominent AMP and Westpac buildings.*

THE TUMULT and shouting had hardly died down along the rocky shores of Narragansett Bay, Newport, Rhode Island on 26 September 1983 when thousands of stunned Americans started asking 'Where the hell is Perth, anyway?' Good question. Famed American television newscaster Walter Cronkite found the city last year and he'll tell you 'Perth is the best-kept secret in the world — it's just beautiful'.

Now that Perth is the new home of the America's Cup — yachting's, nay sport's, most prestigious trophy — Australia's sunniest city is suddenly a vacation destination for thousands of Americans, English and Europeans

And the twenty-sixth defence of the cup has attracted twenty-four challengers from eight nations. If only fifteen or sixteen challengers get their yachts wet off Perth's port of Fremantle, the first defence outside America will still be three times as big as any previous showdown.

Arguably Australia's prettiest capital — most of the argument will come from Sydney — Perth has a population of nearly 950 000, yet it is preparing to play host to about a million visitors over the next two years. And the Western Australian Tourism Commission estimates the cup defence will bring revenues totalling $1500 million to the sparsely populated state, which sandgropers — the colloquial name for West Aussies — hasten to point out is three times the size of Texas.

So Perth, which nestles comfortably along the banks of the picturesque Swan River, the wide expanses of which have spawned a city of yachtsmen, has achieved worldwide notoriety chiefly because a 12-metre yacht called *Australia II*, owned by a self-made mega-millionaire named Alan Bond, wrested the America's Cup from the New York Yacht Club, which had been enjoying sport's longest winning streak: 132 years.

Like the rest of Australia, the western third of the continent was discovered by sailors and explored by them as far as its rivers were navigable. The west coast is strewn with the wrecks of seventeenth-century Dutch East Indies galleons, which tracked the path of the Roaring Forties from the Cape of Good Hope across the Indian Ocean before turning northwards to Batavia (now Jakarta). Many failed to turn northwards in time and fine ships like the *Gilt Dragon*, *Zeewyck*, *Zuytdorp* and *Batavia* crashed onto offshore reefs or low limestone/coral islands.

Western Australia was settled through its natural harbours and its rivers provided the first inland roads. A Dutch navigator, Willem de Vlamingh, was the first to explore the Swan River, and he named it for the vast numbers of black swans he sighted on its pleasant reaches. But it was not till nearly two centuries later that Captain James Stirling, a British sea captain, recognised the potential of the river mouth as a harbour and the river itself as a watery highway to grassy banks upstream.

Stirling decided it was the perfect bridgehead for a new British colony and on 2 May 1829, Captain Fremantle annexed the western third of Australia for Britain. The port of Fremantle was born, and a few months later, on 12 August, the town of Perth was established 18 kilometres upstream by the cutting down of a tree by a soldier's wife on a site near where convicts would later build the town hall.

As the twin towns evolved, suburban development grew along interconnecting roads and railways, at river landings and along roads radiating to out-settlements of the colony.

Situated as it is on the western seaboard, about 2000 kilometres from Adelaide, the nearest of the other state capitals, Perth is the nation's most isolated capital, a fact of life that used to bother a lot of West Australians. But no more. Perth people generally enjoy a lifestyle that would be hard to duplicate in any other part of Australia.

Most West Australians travel to South-East Asia for holidays rather than to the eastern capitals, and many travel to Europe and the United States. But, because of their isolation, Perth people are noted for their warmth and friendliness, a trait for which they have a national and international reputation.

Their parochial pride got a kick where it most hurts when a top Sydney architect visited the city-on-the-Swan and described Perth's buildings as crude, clumsy and badly designed. Nevile Gruzman declared that the western capital was heading towards becoming the ugliest city in Australia. 'I can only believe your architects are letting you down badly', Gruzman said, adding that he believed that many of the buildings in the city should be demolished and a fresh start made.

Of course, his remarks brought reactions that ranged from scorn to outright outrage from its proud citizens, not to mention its architects, some of whom had won national awards for their designs. The West Australian branch of the Royal Australian Institute of Architects criticised Gruzman's allegations as insubstantial and unspecific and pointed out that he had 'no particular expertise in high-rise development'.

Let's zoom in on Perth, the central business district of which is built on a gently sloping north bank of the Swan.

The business heart of Perth is found along wide, tree-lined St George's Terrace and its eastern extension, Adelaide Terrace. Here, tall concrete and glass buildings rear incongruously alongside more traditional buildings put up in the city's early days. Hardly a month passes without a solid old six- or seven-storey building being demolished to make way for a skyscraper — or what passes for one in Perth. The terrace's bigger buildings have created something of a wind tunnel along which, for half of the year, the morning easterlies and the afternoon sea breeze blow with great gusto.

The next street north of the terrace is Hay Street, one long block of which has been turned into a tree-dotted and flower-boxed decorative mall. Hay Street is the city's shopping centre,

Above: *Looking south-west from the city across the Narrows Bridge and Kings Park to Fremantle in the distance.*

Right: *The Mitchell Freeway sweeps into the city across the Narrows Bridge separating Perth Water and Melville Water. Below the bridge is the Entertainment Centre and to the left, the city centre.*

supplemented by the next two parallel streets, Murray Street and Wellington Street. Most of the shops and department stores in Hay, Murray and Wellington streets are low-rise and shopping arcades link these thoroughfares to St George's Terrace.

Perth clings to its convict past and several buildings hark back to the days when miscreants from the United Kingdom were imprisoned in the colony. Perth's Town Hall, at the corner of Hay Street and Barrack Street, is a fine example of a convict-built edifice; it even has broad arrows built into the brickwork. The colony was not founded as a convict settlement, however. Captain Stirling had returned from England in 1829 with the first load of settlers in a ship called the *Parmelia,* a name that has been bestowed on the international-standard Parmelia Hilton Hotel. The convicts came later to work the sand-loam soils along the banks of the Swan and Avon rivers and help build the town itself.

At the western end of St George's Terrace, just below Perth's Parliament House, is the towered archway of what, in colonial times, was the Army barracks. The old convict-built barracks was demolished in the face of furious opposition, and the government of the time compromised by leaving the archway intact. Though it looks incongruous, it has satisfied the traditionalists.

A tourist drawcard in central Perth is London Court, an Elizabethan-style courtyard linking Hay Street with St George's

Central Perth retains a green and parklike quality. The war memorial in Kings Park (above) *is close by the intersecting tentacles of the Mitchell Freeway* (below). *Behind Parliament House and the Barracks Arch (right), St George's Terrace leads to the city.*

GRIFFIN
CityMutual

Terrace. It has a clocktower at either end on which St George and the dragon joust every hour on the hour.

The future growth of the central business district is restricted in the south by the Swan River, in the north by the central railway system and in the west by the Mitchell Freeway, which snakes out to the western and northern 'mortgage belts'. This has resulted in the construction of many high-rise buildings, some of which no doubt led to Gruzman's criticism.

Perth's architecture is that of a European society grafted to a strange and rugged land. It is not an indigenous architecture evolving from primitivism, but rather an adaptation of developed, introduced forms to local conditions designed to accommodate established living patterns. The colonial society was essentially British and the city's architecture followed British styling till well into the twentieth century.

In the early 1890s a gold boom on the West Australian goldfields around Coolgardie and Kalgoorlie brought a remarkable change to the face of Perth. Coupled with a recession in the eastern colonies, the gold rush brought a flood of academically qualified architects and master builders to the western capital.

Perth and Fremantle were virtually rebuilt in less than twenty years, and the architecture of improvisation and pattern books was replaced by the eclecticism and invention of professionals. Edwardian classicism and late Victorian architecture predomi-

Right: *The Merlin, one of Perth's new generation international hotels.*

Below: *Beatty Park Aquatic Centre, Leaderville, swimming venue for the 1962 Commonwealth Games.*

nated and there was a splashing of the Italianate style imported from Victoria. The architectural impact of the gold boom can be seen throughout the western capital today alongside buildings of the 'modern movement', which was supported by the nickel and iron ore mining booms of the sixties and seventies. Perth's most effervescent building is probably His Majesty's Theatre at the corner of Hay and King Streets. Built in 1903–04 it has a facade that comes alive with romanesque balconies and stucco icing. One of the original gold-rush buildings still standing is the Palace Hotel (c. 1895) at the corner of St George's Terrace and William Street. A skyscraper office block is being built on this prime site by the Bond Corporation, which plans to retain the old hotel — as a bank — in the foreground. Another of the older hotels, the Savoy, still stands in all its opulence in Hay Street, with balconies providing grandstands to activities on the mall outside.

Most of Perth's so-called 'modern movement' buildings are located on St George's Terrace or its continuation, Adelaide Terrace. The city's most distinguished edifice is Allendale Square, a high-rise office tower clad in anodised aluminium panels. A building of high environmental impact in a crisp, modern technological style, it has won four top awards, including the Royal Australian Institute of Architects' design award for 1978.

Almost opposite Allendale is the St Martins Centre, three office towers with pedestrian concourses, built in reinforced concrete in a restrained style. The handsome building maximises on panoramic views, pedestrian spaces and arcade links to the commercial centre of the city. Further down the terrace, at the intersection of William Street and opposite the Palace Hotel, is the Westpac Building, a high-rise reinforced concrete office tower. A modern commercial redevelopment in the international style of the early seventies, it was built for a bank — formerly the Bank of New Sout Wales — that has occupied the site since early Victorian days.

In Adelaide Terrace in downtown Perth is one of Perth's newer hotels, the Merlin, which is a complex of high-rise hotel with shopping arcades and provision for future office towers. Crisp, brick-clad armatures supporting curved glass roofs over circulation spaces reflect the spirit of America's Portman in its handling of multi-storeyed atriums.

On its doorstep Perth has a natural bushland park that is the envy of every other Australian capital. Kings Park, just west of the city and encompassing Mount Eliza, which rears up from the banks of the Swan River near the old Swan Brewery (soon to be redeveloped), is nearly 450 hectares of natural bushland and wildflowers interspersed with a fine botanical garden, playgrounds and lookouts. In 1895, in a brilliant act of foresight, Sir John Forrest's government set aside the land for public use, and despite moves — which were thwarted — to build cultural venues and an Olympic pool there, it has remained basically the same as it was nearly a century ago.

Right: *Ascot racecourse, on which the Australian Derby and Perth Cup are run.*

Above: *Government House, built between 1859 and 1864. Its turrets and arches are reminiscent of those of the Tower of London.*

Below: *City station and central bus terminal, Wellington Steet.*

SHERATON

Pages 176–177: *Looking east along St George's Terrace to Adelaide Terrace. In the foreground are St Andrew's Uniting Church on the left and Government House on the right.*

Above: *Looking north-west. Lake Monger is in the background, far left, and the Entertainment Centre is in the middle distance.*

BOND
FINANCE

From a war memorial on the edge of Mt Eliza and its surrounding lawns, Perth people and their visitors can get a fine panorama of the city and the Swan River. From the memorial, paths lead down the slopes of the mount to a spring where a fountain was built in 1861, from a design by Royal Engineer R.G. Thorold.

The city-on-the-Swan has many fine parks and gardens. Government House Gardens, established in 1887, and situated alongside the Perth Concert Hall, were laid out around the then new Government House between St George's Terrace and reclaimed river flats. The garden has mostly exotic trees and shrubs. West Australian governor, Professor Gordon Reid, and his wife are throwing open the gardens more and more to the public.

Perth's earliest gardens, established in 1844, is Stirling Gardens, which was set aside for the cultivation and acclimatisation of introduced species as well as for public enjoyment. Among Australia's finest, it is a lunch-hour refuge for hundreds of terrace office workers.

Hyde Park is built around one of several freshwater lakes that occur north of the city. Landscaped, like Government House Gardens, in the romantic tradition, it has exotic trees surrounding twin lakes that contain island refuges for wildfowl.

Just over the Narrows Bridge in South Perth is the Perth Zoological Gardens, a 20-hectare oasis amid high-rise apartments and suburban housing.

Queens Gardens was developed at East Perth from 1899 on the site of a former brickworks clay quarry, again in the English romantic tradition with sculpted natural water pools. A feature is a sculpture of Peter Pan, a replica of Sir George Frampton's work in Kensington Gardens, London.

Perth people inevitably show their visitors their beloved University of Western Australia at Crawley, a few kilometres from the city. Built in the Mediterranean tradition, the campus is a fine example of the integration of buildings and landscape. It has been claimed that the humanistic formality and Mediterranean repose of the campus has a mood-controlling effect on its students and contributes to the relatively low level of student demonstrations. It has many landscaped venues for cultural events, including a sunken garden, an outdoor theatre called Somerville Auditorium and the Octagon Theatre. Perth has two other tertiary education centres: the West Australian Institute of Technology and the Murdoch University.

The Perth metropolitan area is noted for its garden suburbs. With the return of ex-servicemen from World War II, a building boom saw new suburban subdivision burgeoning in what was once virgin bushland. The Garden City Movement made its presence felt, especially in City Beach, Floreat, South Perth and, to a lesser degree, in Mount Lawley. Since 1976, the trend has been to the northern suburbs and new beach subdivisions like Carine, Whitfords and Sorrento. Unfenced and reticulated lawns are de rigueur in these garden suburbs.

Pages 180–181 and below right: *Australia Day celebrations.*

Pages 184–185: *Heirisson Island is crossed by bridge and causeway. On the right is the WACA, home of the Western Australian Cricket Association and one of Australia's most attractive cricket grounds.*

Above right: *South-west of the city, the Canning Bridge crosses the Canning River, a tributary of the Swan.*

Below: *Patterns on the Swan, as a Rottnest Island ferry crosses the path of a pleasure boat.*

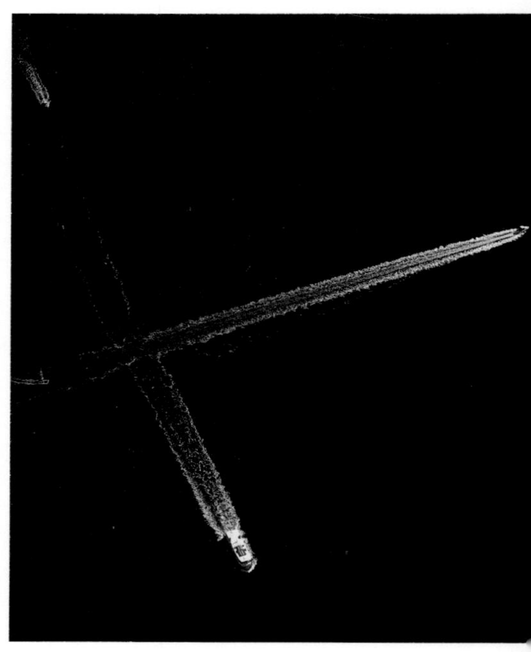

Perth's climate and river location make it ideal for water sports. The expanse of water surrounding the city can be gauged from the photograph above which shows South Perth, looking along the Swan River to the Indian Ocean.

Left: *The Western Australian Lawn Tennis Association's courts, Kings Park.*

Most of Perth's many self-made millionaires — the city is sometimes called the Dallas of Australia — live in the posher suburbs of Dalkeith, Peppermint Grove and Mosman Park. One thoroughfare in Dalkeith, Jutland Parade, is Perth's 'Millionaires' Row' and is reputed to be Australia's richest street. Set on one of the prettiest stretches of the Swan River, Jutland Parade boasts some of the finest homes in Western Australia, ranging from charming art deco houses to modern concrete and glass mansions.

Perth's smallest suburb, Peppermint Grove, which is only about a hundred hectares, is also favoured by millionaires, and most of its mansions are architect-designed. Sitting atop Keane's Point in the Grove is one of Perth's tiniest yacht clubs, Royal Freshwater Bay.

Because of its fine climate — a year-round average of eight hours of sunshine a day — and river heritage, Perth boasts several yacht clubs. They include the Royal Perth Yacht Club, under whose burgee Alan Bond captured the America's Cup. The ornate Victorian pitcher, once called the Hundred-Guinea Cup, now stands in a burgundy velvet-lined bullet-proof glass case in a semi-private upstairs lounge. One metre outside the case a brass plaque is set into the floor proclaiming that the America's Cup would be bolted to the plaque in 1980. It was put there by optimistic club members three years too early. As he photographed the plaque, Walter Cronkite quipped, 'This plate will be redundant after 1987'.

Suburban patterns: rectangular grids (right) *and special-purpose cluster housing* (below). *Hyde Park, in Highgate, provides a wooded green retreat for the northern suburbs.*

Royal Perth, which has nearly 2000 members, is charmingly set on Pelican Point, a favourite birdwatching spot of the Duke of Edinburgh on his visits to Australia. Pelican Point is at the western end of Crawley Bay, only a few kilometres from the city. Yacht club members and their guests look through a forest of masts across the river to the city skyline.

The big yacht clubs — one of the biggest is south of Perth — hold weekly twilight sailing races around the river, starting around 6 p.m. and finishing in darkness. Noted more for the number of female 'crew' and the volumes of champagne and beer consumed than for any compulsion to actually try to win, these races are a growing part of Perth's summer scene.

Winter or summer, the social fabric of Perth is woven around outdoor entertainment: barbecues and pool parties are popular summer night activities in the balmy Mediterranean climate; more and more restaurants are introducing garden and street-front outdoor settings. The growth of pavement restaurants has been inhibited, however, by the ubiquitous *Musca domestica*, the common house fly. One of the minuses of living in Perth is the number of flies. The 'West Australian salute' — continual waving of one or both hands across the face — is a long-standing joke in the West.

Perth is a fast-growing city and its suburbs are encroaching on previously agricultural or undeveloped land. A view of the northern suburbs, looking south (right). *Closer to the city, Cottesloe Beach* (below) *is a popular Indian Ocean beach.*

Left: *The West Coast Highway snakes along the Indian Ocean coastline through the northern suburbs.*

Above: *Volley ball at Swanbourne, Perth's nudist beach.*

Perth has more restaurants and nightclubs, on a per capita basis, than any other Australian capital city, more than half of its 1000-plus restaurants are BYOGs — an acronym for 'Bring Your Own Grog'. The Kings Cross of Perth is across the Perth–Fremantle railway line at Northbridge where ethnic restaurants and raunchy nightclubs, featuring some of Australia's top bands, abound. Several Vietnamese restaurants have been established by refugees for the growing number of their own countrymen and for Perth people who like the cuisine and the prices.

Perth is a beachlover's paradise. It has more than 70 kilometres of whiter-than-white unpolluted beaches that stretch from south of Fremantle to Mullaloo and include such beaches as Leighton, Cottesloe, Swanbourne, City Beach, Scarborough and Sorrento. Swanbourne Beach, which overlooks the America's Cup course, is reputedly the biggest nude beach in Australia. Though it lacks amenities such as shops and hotels, Swanbourne attracts up to 5000 nudists a day on hot weekends. Most go there to worship the sun; some to ogle the bare flesh. Not surprisingly, Perth has one of the highest incidences of skin cancer in Australia.

Many of the coastal dunes behind Perth's beaches will be grandstands from which Perthites can watch the America's Cup racing in 1986–87. Most of the America's Cup action will centre around Fremantle — a remarkably intact and unique Victorian town — and nearly all of the America's Cup 12-metre yachts will be accommodated at Fremantle docks in three harbours.

The Fremantle Sailing Club, which has one of the finest yacht-club premises and dockage in the southern hemisphere in Success Harbour, will play host to a few foreign challengers. Several, including the New York Yacht Club, will be accommodated in the adjacent Fremantle Fisherman's Harbour; and the remainder will be docked in a new multi-million-dollar marina being built on the northern end of Fisherman's Harbour.

Fremantle has almost the atmosphere of Newport, Rhode Island, longtime venue for America's Cup racing. It has several fine old limestone buildings, many of them built by convicts who arrived in 1850 to fill a shortage of labour. They include the Round House, the old Mental Asylum (now a maritime museum), Fremantle Gaol, the Commissariat Building and warders' cottages.

But America's Cup afficionados who flock to Fremantle and Perth in 1986–87 will find the sea and weather conditions vastly different from those prevailing off Newport. While the winds over Rhode Island Sound can be flukey and often too light for racing, the afternoon sea breeze — a Sou'wester — that prevails in the summer off Fremantle, averages about 17 knots and blows at up to 30 knots. Perth people call it the 'Fremantle doctor', because it brings welcome relief from the heat.

Perth's healthy climate has spawned a city of sports-lovers, and every weekend myriads of cricketers, hockey players, netballers, baseballers, softballers, tennis players and (in winter) footballers flock to the many fine sportsgrounds dotted round the suburbs. Despite its comparatively small population, Western Australia is currently the champion football state and has held the Sheffield Shield for cricket for seven of the last twelve years. Racing and pacing both thrive in Perth.

As noted earlier, Perth and Fremantle people are known the world over for their warmth and friendliness. Many sociologists attribute this to the cities' isolation from the rest of the world, indeed the rest of Australia; others say it is a natural corollary of having a climate most Californians would envy and an easy-going laid-back lifestyle. Whatever the reason, West Australian America's Cup syndicate executives have warned that over-friendliness could result in a foreign challenger's removing the cup from its glass case at Royal Perth.

But home-grown sandgropers will have none of this. West Australians can no more change their psyche than a tiger can its stripes. And for a city whose fastest-growing industry is tourism, it would be folly for Perthites to give visitors the cold shoulder. It's just not their style.

Fremantle, at the mouth of the Swan River, is the principal seaport of the west and an important industrial centre. Once the largest settlement in Western Australia, Fremantle lost ground to Perth, upriver, but is now being enthusiastically prepared to host the yachts and crews that will vie for the America's Cup in 1987.

Canberra
ROBERT HAUPT

Pages 196–197: *Australia's new Parliament House emerges from Capital Hill. The design, selected from 329 entries in an international competition, is by Mitchell/Giurgola and Thorp, New York.*

Left: *From the Australian War Memorial, Anzac Parade, 'truly a ceremonial way', stretches towards Parliament House, with the Capital Hill site behind it.*

Below: *The Anzac Parade Offices and part of Commonwealth Park where Anzac Parade meets Lake Burley Griffin.*

ONCE THEY HAD decided to build an inland city, the planners of Australia's capital had a great problem. It was one that the early explorers had faced: how to cope with the monotony of the Australian landscape. The building of Canberra, in the 60 years from the surveyors' huts to the city of today, is the story of a battle against the harshness of the Australian landscape, of Europeans civilising the bush. The battle is only half won.

By road, the approaches to Canberra take you through classic Australian countryside; crop and grazing land interspersed with dry scrub. It is a journey that always seems to take a little longer than you expect, as if one or two extra lengths of featureless scenery had been put in along the road since the last time you travelled it. The bend that puts you in sight of Black Mountain tower is for this reason the more eagerly sought, like a lighthouse after an arduous sea voyage. Motorists are welcomed to Canberra with splendid notices and elaborate help; they are always glad to have arrived. It is another manifestation of the problems of that inland site that no one arrives by land wishing that his or her journey had been longer.

From the air, our vantage point, Canberra has two faces. From low altitude, as your plane banks around Mt Ainslie — sometimes so close to it that you can see the faces of the spectators on the lookout there — Canberra reveals the breadth of European change. Suburbs spread from north of Mt Ainslie clear out of sight towards the Murrumbidgee in the south, a distance of over 60 kilometres. In the east, the Belconnen suburbs have grown to virtually surround Black Mountain. This rapid growth in the footprint of European man has mostly occurred since 1970.

Occasionally, however, you might see Canberra from a higher level; perhaps from 11 000 metres on the Sydney – Melbourne run. The picture is different. The man-made marks are indistinct. With no great port or concentration of heavy industry, without skyscrapers or major bridges, Canberra barely appears real; even its lake might, on a hazy day, be a mirage. Its insubstantiality is no doubt in part due to the towering contrast of the Snowy Mountains, but it makes us reflect on how small a mark suburbanisation makes on the Australian landscape. And it is in its suburbanness as much as in its site that Canberra presents a typically Australian face.

Canberra is used to the name 'bush capital'; to residents who have been there long enough, it applies to the days before the lake, when sheep did safely graze within sight of Parliament House. To those who came later, Canberra was a bush capital when the sub-

urbs stopped and the snakes began, about a kilometre past the Prime Minister's Lodge — back when Sir John Gorton, a long-term Canberran, occupied the residence. Later still, around the time of Gough Whitlam, the bush of the bush capital began at the end of the Woden Valley. Today, all would agree, there is much more capital and far less bush, and the name is hardly warranted at all.

But the bush is still closely with us in Canberra, and perhaps the planners were wise to have it that way. The air is dry. When a bushfire is threatening, even the most urbane prime minister — one perfectly at home with diplomats of London and Geneva — will smell the smoke and see the sun blacked out. There are still black snakes near the Lodge. The scrub still gets into untidy view, the soil is yet clearly arid within executive vision, there is a magnificent collection of paspalum; and should these singularities — from the European standpoint, defects — ever be overcome, there will always be the reminder of the bush's hostility in the broad and sullen sky.

The planners' attack on monotony had two fronts: one was to select a basin, with peaks around; the other was to choose, after an international competition, a forward young architect from Chicago to design the city. The combination was a success. Pleased with his basin, Walter Burley Griffin filled it with pleasing prospects. His bold plan stands out from the air, like a piece of horizontal art-deco, in circles, straight lines and sharp angles. Canberra's early buildings were similarly geometrical. It all seems rather old-fashioned now, but Canberra's initial design had an answer for the monotony problem: open up vistas.

So gums were felled and the red dirt was scraped into boulevards. Paris might be far away, but the principles of that cityscape, so much admired in the nineteenth and early twentieth centuries, were as applicable on the Molonglo's banks as on the Seine's. Entry to the infant capital was made by a grand march up the (still to be grandly named) Northbourne Avenue, and the city's axis was put between Parliament House and the Australian War Memorial along the parade named to honour Australia's first, still-fresh, unifying myth: Anzac.

These days, Northbourne is an undistinguished thoroughfare — a road, not a parade. Visitors who drive along it expecting to be impressed by the capital's well-known landmarks see instead a dreary line of flats hiding behind bushes. Attempts have been made to manicure its untidy bush fringes, but they haven't come to much. Northbourne Avenue doesn't even take you to town; visitors are liable to scoot around City Hill and be halfway across Commonwealth Bridge before they realise that the city centre (to the locals, 'Civic') is behind them.

Left: *Burley Griffin's design 'stands out from the air, like a piece of horizontal art-deco, in circles, straight lines and sharp angles'. A view from Regatta Point towards City Hill.*

Above: *Civic Centre, Canberra's first administrative and commercial centre. Its earliest buildings (1927) are now dwarfed by more modern business houses.*

Left: *Commonwealth Avenue Bridge, spanning Lake Burley Griffin.*

Right: *Northbourne Avenue, the main thoroughfare into Canberra from the north, with the Canberra International Hotel in the foreground.*

Pages 204–205: *The War Memorial, Anzac Parade and Parliament House on the left; Commonwealth Avenue Bridge, centre; and Civic to the right.*

Anzac Parade is quite different. This is truly a ceremonial way, an avenue designed more to be looked at than driven on. Its purpose is specific, its design clear and its execution splendid. What Anzac Parade is there to do is to catch the eye of every person leaving Parliament House and direct it to the Australian War Memorial. It works every time, though to what effect in an era of disarmament politics it is not easy to say. Still, a legislator is forced to *see* the war memorial every time he walks out of the parliament. For anyone who has worked at Parliament House for any length of time, that grey-green building with its squat dome becomes a fixture in the mind, a kind of unblinking eye that supervises your departure, night and day. All because of Anzac Parade.

Parliament House, old and new. The original building (above), *always intended as 'provisional', was opened in May 1927. The permanent Parliament House* (right) *will be opened in 1988, Australia's bicentennial year. According to those who selected it, the design 'is a building of firm, clear geometry, not rigidly imposed on the terrain but sensitively adjusted to it'.*

But Burley Griffin's squares and circles were abandoned as Canberra grew. They apply only in the older — today the smaller but by far the more important — part of town. Essentially, the foundation of the city's design moved from the nineteenth to the twentieth century. The agent of change was the motor car. In Burley Griffin's geometrical design intersections abounded, some of them perplexing clusters where roads met on the circle, tangent and square, and hazard confronted you at five or more angles simultaneously. The residential streets were laid out in grids — again, maximising the potential for collison. Those most at risk, of course, are the visitors, who are generally to be found parked to the side of one of these intersectional puzzles, consulting a map.

Left: *The Australian–American Memorial, built by public subscription and unveiled in 1954, commemorates the contribution of the United States to Australia's defence in World War II.*

Below: *The National Library of Australia, opened in 1968, houses a vast collection of books, maps, photographs and films.*

Right: *The Carillon on Aspen Island, a gift from the British government to mark Canberra's fiftieth anniversary, contains fifty-three bells and is among the largest in the world.*

The Australian War Memorial is a shrine, art gallery and museum. Opened in 1941, it is a stylised Byzantine building surmounted by a copper dome over the Hall of Memory.

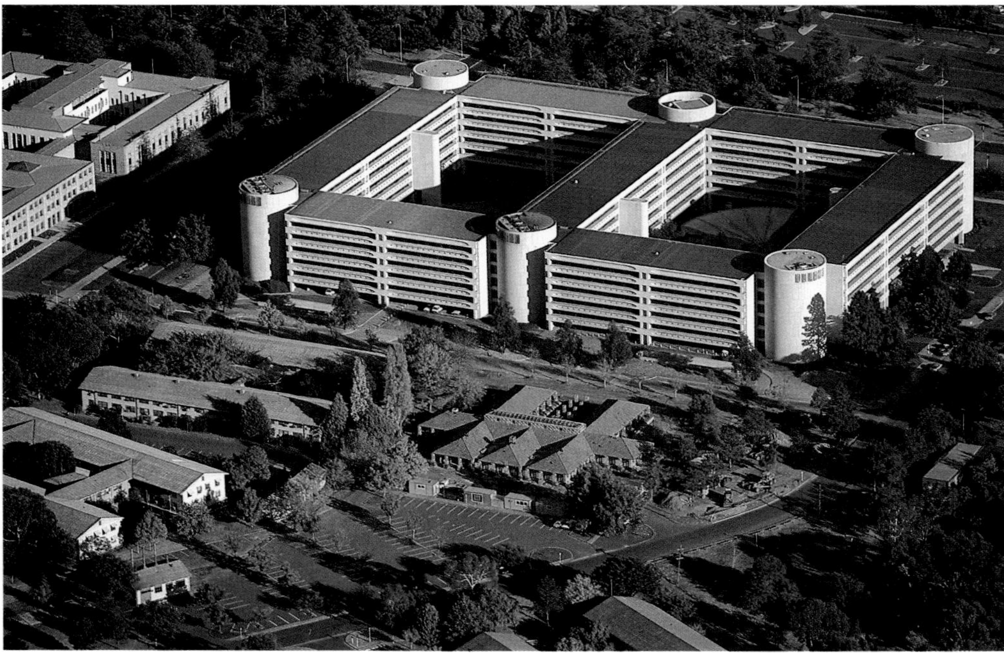

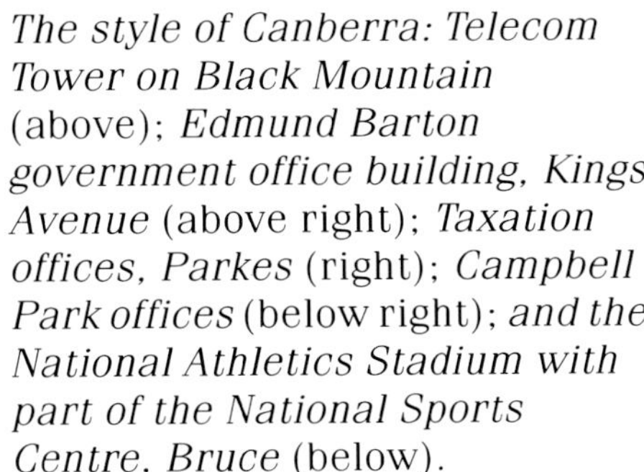

The style of Canberra: Telecom Tower on Black Mountain (above); *Edmund Barton government office building, Kings Avenue* (above right); *Taxation offices, Parkes* (right); *Campbell Park offices* (below right); *and the National Athletics Stadium with part of the National Sports Centre, Bruce* (below).

Above: *Benjamin government offices at Belconnen, one of several satellite towns around Canberra. These towns, virtually self-contained, were built to avoid the excessive centralisation and rapid unplanned growth of other cities.*

Left: *Well-established suburbia. 'All over Canberra it is the street that counts: its aspect, quietness and, particularly, elevation.'*

Above right: *Queanbeyan, across the border in New South Wales, has developed more haphazardly than neighbouring Canberra.*

Right: *Shackleton Park, Mawson.*

Far right: *Argyle Square, Reid.*

In the sixties, the planners threw away the set square, compass and ruler and began building the suburbs, ants'-nest style, around a hierarchy of roads in which cul-de-sacs lead to wriggly avenues, avenues to crescents and crescents on to arterial roads. These major roads, clearly visible from the air, are the business end of the Canberra road system. Carrying the heavy traffic that is such a burden in the older cities, they sweep around a suburb, bundle it up and deliver it, wrapped, to a freeway. In the newer part of Canberra the suburbs sit along the freeways like presents on the branch of a Christmas tree.

It is a solution not without cost. Each of these suburbs has a characteristic aspect, and it is the same aspect: the curving road bordered by well-mown nature strips. Sometimes the road will disappear over a hill; at other places it hides coyly behind trees or in the garden bushes. The effect can be oppressive: so many blind corners, so many neat lawns, so little variety.

Using the freeways, you may swing quickly from one suburb clear across town to another with no jams; that's the advantage of rational town planning. The cost is that the place you will arrive in differs in no significant visible way from the place you left. The defining characteristic of Canberra is its sameness. That is what visitors mean when they say it is 'artificial' (after all, every city is a human artifice; it is just that the less a city is planned, the more it resembles an organism). Perhaps that sameness is apt, in the capital city of a country dedicated to equality.

The car rules Canberra, OK? This is a city in which kerbs and guttering, streets and even freeways are built in anticipation of tomorrow's motoring. Were it tropical, Canberra would look, at its extremities, like a city that was petering out. In fact, at the point where its bitumen meets the stalky grass of the plains Canberra is petering *in*. It could, left alone, peter across half the Monaro plain without leaving the Capital Territory, and are the politicians who seized Capital Hill the ones to stop it? Canberra's lichen has not crossed the Murrumbidgee. The day that it does will be a milestone.

Until quite recently, when Canberra expanded it did so bacterially, by increasing its stock of almost-identical cells. The pressure of population, which accounts for most of the good and the bad things of city life was, thus, curiously transmuted in Canberra. Hardly another city anywhere better fitted Alan Coren's witty description of the outcome of modern planning: 'a suburb without an urb'. The pressure that overflows from a suburb — the tide of people looking for work, shops, colleges or a good night out — was deliberately contained within Canberra's 'town centres': Woden, Belconnen, Weston and Ginninderra. They prospered in the name of keeping Canberra's real centre, Civic, from overcrowding, traffic congestion, pollution and the other evils of real-city life.

Canberra people alone can say whether the cost of this — the endless, urb-less suburb surrounding a centre that is virtually empty by 9 p.m. — has been too great. In one respect, they may

Right: *Royal Military College, Duntroon, built on land first settled by merchant Robert Campbell. Founded, on Lord Kitchener's recommendation, in 1911, Duntroon is Australia's oldest services college.*

Below: *Royal Canberra Golf Course.*

Pages 214–215: *Looking south across Lake Burley Griffin towards Woden Town Centre. Black Mountain Peninsula is on the left; Weston Park Peninsula in the centre.*

already be giving their answer. Although Canberra still grows mainly horizontally, like lichen, it has recently begun to bunch up in some of the older suburbs and develop density. The rents and prices of townhouses in Kingston show the demand for an alternative to the three-bedroom cottage on the quarter-acre block. A high-rise residential unit called Kingston Towers is now going up; when it is finished Canberra people will be found for the first time living at such heady heights as the twelfth floor. Though it isn't on any tour schedules, Kingston Towers is for the historian of Canberra life one of the city's more significant buildings.

The building that will set Australia buzzing — with delight and indignation — is growing steadily, like scar-tissue in a wound, from the centre of a hole as big as a mine on Capital Hill. Scar-tissue is an apt metaphor for the new Parliament House that will open in 1988, given the years of controversy and debate it has already caused. At one point in the early seventies the two chambers of parliament were divided: the Senate voting to go down by the lake; the House of Representatives opting for Burley Griffin's site, the small rise behind the current House.

Seldom has the site of an Australian building had such an interesting psychological history. In the debates that rambled on about the replacement House, a formidable argument was deployed against the lakeside site: floods. True, flooding would be rare, but the mere thought of it drove the legislature and the executive (which together could control their destiny) to cede the lakeside site to the judiciary and the arts (which could not). The High Court and the National Gallery now sit at water's edge; they must cope with whatever torrents Nature may see fit to send down the Molonglo, while parliament watches safely from on high.

A smoky haze filters the light as bushfire burns around Canberra. Scrivener Dam (left) *holds back the waters of the Molonglo River to form Lake Burley Griffin. A site near the dam has been designated for the new Museum of Australia.*

Although there was once a vote from one chamber to fulfil Burley Griffin's plan, there was never much enthusiasm for his site. Camp Hill, a scrubby mound behind the current Parliament House that houses a staff car park. Although it was not said in so many words, the parliamentarians yearned for something more conspicuous.

Capital Hill was the only other site seriously considered and the psychological resistance to it was strong at first. Some members asserted that it would be presumptous for the representatives of the people to put themselves above the people. This was egalitarianism, the oldest rallying cry in Australian politics, and it took patience to overcome it. But after Prime Minister Malcolm Fraser set the goal of a new Parliament House for the Bicentenary in 1988, Capital Hill was taken and sliced open. The parliamentary tribute to egalitarianism survived (with a touch of practicality in this nuclear age) in the choice of a design that puts the bulk of the building beneath ground level. The new Parliament House will be *in* Capital Hill as much as *on* it. It will be a high-security House, with entrances that shield arriving politicians from the public. To the occupants of the new Parliament House, Anzac Parade will beckon mostly in vain.

One cannot consider Canberra only as a capital, or even as a city. To do the first would be to ignore the thousands for whom parliamentary drama and public-service intrigue might as well be happening in Hollywood: people who work as builders, shop assistants, solicitors or singers and whose living is, accordingly, only incidental to their being Canberrans. Non-political Canberra is growing fast. Its engines are construction, commerce and service; its home, as often as not, lies across the border in Queanbeyan.

Queanbeyan is Canberra's Tijuana, a place of utility and convenience where zoning and building codes are less strict and the roads wander in what, to a Canberra eye, seems haphazard confusion. Looking at the two, you would say Queanbeyan was the poor relation, but just as there is more purchasing-power in some of the unfashionable western suburbs of Sydney and Melbourne than in the posher east, so Queanbeyan hides some fortunes while Canberra hides overdrafts.

To an unusual degree for an Australian city, in Canberra your address announces your status. It's not just a matter of Red Hill, Forrest and Deakin — the lush fastness between Parliament and the Red Hill lookout — being the choice suburbs; all over Canberra, it is the street that counts: its aspect, quietness and, particularly, elevation. Like the divisions and grades of the career public service, the tiers of Canberra's suburbs reflect the twin yardsticks of achievement: status and wealth.

To live in Queanbeyan, on the other hand, is to renounce all that. It is a place that doesn't mind showing its rough edges. Some of the politicians of more modest means rent accommodation there, to escape the oppressive rents of Canberra.

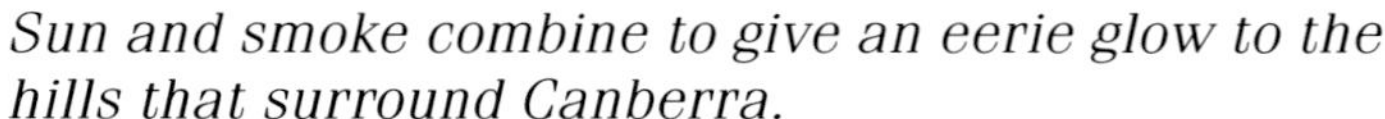

Sun and smoke combine to give an eerie glow to the hills that surround Canberra.

'The bush is still closely with us in Canberra . . . The air is dry. When a bushfire is threatening, even the most urbane prime minister will smell the smoke and see the sun blacked out.' Fire surrounds the national capital, March 1985.

Walter Burley Griffin is commemorated today in the name of the lake, which provides the field for the vistas he established along the axes: Capital Hill–Civic, Capital Hill–Russell and, central to the whole design, Parliament House–War Memorial. This remains the Canberra of the picture postcards, the scenic focus of the city.

But to the east, the north and, particularly, the south, the suburbs have escaped his grid and proliferated in a style that at first seems looser but which, in fact, has merely substituted one kind of rigidity for another. The waters of Lake Burley Griffin are in places deceptively shallow. The psyche of Canberra — such a well-regulated place from the air, with a place for every house and every house in its place — might follow the opposite rule. Novels are being written — more important, being set — here in these tidy suburbs. The texture is thickening, the cringe is weakening. When the sun rises over Black Mountain on 26 January 1988 to announce the beginning of Australia's second European century, will we be finally ready to believe that the bush capital has come of age?

Hobart

ROSS GATES

SBT

Pages 228–229: *Dusk over Hobart; Wrest Point left foreground, the Tasman Bridge to the right.*

Left: *Looking north-east to the city, with part of South Hobart in the foreground.*

Below: *St David's Cathedral and the public buildings of the city centre.*

VISITORS to Hobart and former residents often jokingly refer to the city's traffic problems as the 'peak minute'. Unlike the capitals to the north the Southern Belle does not have to cope with stop–start snarls morning and night. Commuters spill across the five-lane Tasman Bridge and others are funnelled into the city by northern and southern expressways, but there is seldom a hitch in the flow.

They still talk about the morning bus drivers went out on strike (suburban trains were phased out years ago); there were no jams and everyone got to work on time. Some thought the traffic flowed better without the buses and the drivers were back at work the next day.

The peak minute is one of the reasons so many people are happy living in the deep south and for the growing number of Sydney and Melbourne dwellers who have retired and headed for Hobart. It's an easier lifestyle with fewer hassles and realistic prices for houses and property.

In recent times the Tasmanian government, in an effort to lift the almost static population growth, has promoted this concept in the bigger mainland cities. The argument has been simple: sell your $300 000 home in Sydney, buy a better one for $100 000 in Hobart and invest the rest — 200 000 persuasive reasons.

But the beauty of Hobart goes far deeper than dollars and after almost a lifetime of living in Australia's southernmost capital one's appreciation of it continues to grow — enhanced by travel interstate and overseas. Many compare it to Hong Kong, with its majestic Mt Wellington hovering like a silent guardian 1 200 metres above the city, and the Derwent River meandering to the sea.

The river is the lifeblood of the city. Cascading out of the Central Highlands, it slows appreciably 20 kilometres north of Hobart at the small village of New Norfolk, which could have been plucked straight from the English countryside. It is here that the ribbon development begins along both sides of the river; and so too does the love–hate relationship between industry and the residents. Australian Newsprint Mills has a plant at Boyer, just south of New Norfolk and, like the Electrolytic Zinc Company works at Risdon, near Hobart, they have copped criticism in recent years over river pollution. Although both are major employers, the people demanded, and got, a cleaner river and in recent years, the fish have returned in reasonable numbers.

The Derwent's first encounter with the city is the northernmost suburb of Bridgewater where old and new have combined in a rather startling contrast. The old liftspan bridge seems to be guarding the approach to the city while the Housing Department's broadacre development — 'little boxes on the hillside' as that song so quaintly puts it — is hardly a flattering introduction to Hobart.

City perspectives: down Elizabeth Street towards the docks (top left); *upriver towards the Tasman Bridge* (left); *and from the docks to the city centre and beyond* (above).

Pages 234–235: *Panorama of the city and the eastern shore of the Derwent.*

The river continues south past Austins Ferry and then to Claremont, where it sweeps around the peninsula on which Cadburys built its chocolate factory in 1925 and tried to establish a Utopian industrial estate — in those days, a fairly revolutionary concept. Although the plan was never fully realised the idea has survived and the factory nestles among parkland and the pine tree-lined Claremont Golf Club, one of four metropolitan courses around the city. They are international-class courses and the Tasmanian Club, near the Hobart airport, was rated by Sydney golf journalist Tom Ramsay as among the top ten in Australia. Like most of the city's recreational facilities, golf courses are plentiful and members never have to travel more than twenty minutes. The river plays a big part in the recreational life of Hobart which would have the largest number of boat owners, per capita, in Australia. Most backyards have a craft of some description, from swish fibreglass speedboats with monstrous outboards to the lightweight sailboards which are often seen skimming across the Derwent in a fresh sea breeze.

Past Claremont, the river winds through Glenorchy, the centre of the northern sprawl, whose backstreet warehouses and smoking chimneys make it clear this is a working-class area with few pretensions of grandeur. Although Glenorchy has gained city status, it has always lived in the shadow of Hobart and is still regarded by most as part of greater Hobart.

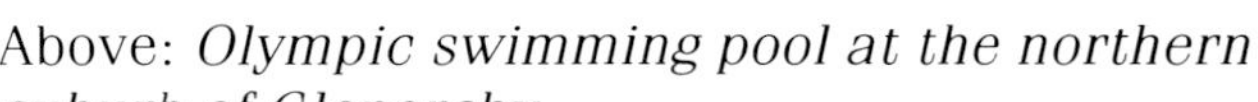

Above: *Olympic swimming pool at the northern suburb of Glenorchy.*

Below: *Franklin Square, a peaceful retreat in the heart of the city.*

Above and below: *Urban symmetry — the Hobart roundabout and its surrounds.*

Like a beacon, the white tower of Wrest Point dominates Sandy Bay. Opened in 1973 as Australia's first legal casino, the hotel complex is a centre of elegance and sophistication.

Glenorchy's link with the eastern shore is the Bowen Bridge, which was completed in 1983 — the final chapter in the Tasman Bridge disaster. It was the evening of 5 January 1975, that the ore carrier *Lake Illawarra* crashed into the Tasman Bridge, creating a hundred-metre chasm which took three years to repair. It divided the city; 50 000 residents in the dormitory suburbs on the eastern shore were stranded and unable to get to work. An armada of ferries, bought and borrowed from overseas and Sydney, were used in the early days after the disaster; later the Army built a bailey bridge, a temporary two-lane crossing about five kilometres upstream from the Tasman Bridge.

Despite the wrench the residents coped and got used to their ferry trips home at night, especially the pint or two of beer at the licensed bar on the boats. But when the Tasman Bridge was reopened it was back on the buses and the colourful ferry saga ended. The Bowen Bridge, near the site of the bailey bridge, was the four-lane 'insurance policy' against another *Lake Illawarra* episode. Although the Tasman Bridge has now been repaired, motorists, as a precaution, must stop at either end of the bridge while a ship passes under.

The relatively new Bowen Bridge is a short stroll from the first settlement of the city, a swampy area Lieutenant Bowen first settled in 1803. His successor, Lieutenant Collins, changed the site further downstream when he arrived the following year. It was a wise move because it proved to be one of the world's best deepwater ports and now has one of the most efficient cargo-handling operations in the country.

It is the Hobart waterfront, with its countless old sandstone buildings, that is the heart of the city. The beauty of Salamanca Place, a popular market for tourists each Saturday, is the essence of the port. It was here the men from the square riggers worked and relaxed. Many of them lived a short walk away at Battery Point, now a popular and highly priced residential area with its beautiful old homes and narrow winding streets.

On the other side of the port are the Henry Jones buildings where Henry Jones established the fruit and jam processing empire that was to stretch as far as South Africa with his IXL label. Although Jones was a takeover victim the Elders-IXL company has emerged as one of the leaders of Australian industry. The state government has gradually renovated the old Jones buildings to retain the character of the waterfront.

When a plan to build an eighteen-storey glass and chrome international hotel on the waterfront was announced the politicians were startled by the reaction. Although fairly conservative, Hobart residents soon showed they would not tolerate any tampering with their maritime heritage. They wanted an international hotel on the waterfront to blend in with the existing buildings. Hobart is the second oldest capital city in Australia and the residents have become acutely aware of its historical importance. They are determined to retain Hobart's salty sandstone exterior.

Above: *Elizabeth Mall.*

Below: *Waterman's Dock at Fiesta time.*

Right: *Looking up the Derwent towards Lindisfarne on the eastern shore.*

SEAFAST
H. JONES & CO. PTY LTD
I.X.L. JAMS
FRESH FISH

The end of the Sydney–Hobart yacht race is a time for celebration; the yachts at anchor are a colourful source of interest for the passing crowds.

Left: *Victoria Dock and the historic Henry Jones buildings along the waterfront.*

Right: *Government House, completed in 1858, in the Domain on the western foreshores of the Derwent.*

Left: *The Shot Tower at Taroona, south of the city on the Channel Highway.*

Below: *Contrasts in suburban lifestyles are graphically illustrated from the air.*

Despite their conservatism Hobartians have gradually become aware of the importance of conservation. This has been highlighted in recent years by the battle between conservationists and the establishment over the flooding of Lake Pedder and more recently, the proposed Gordon-below-Franklin electricity scheme. Lake Pedder was flooded but the conservationists, or 'greenies' as they were dubbed, grabbed international attention when they stopped the flooding of the wild Franklin River. Hobart was the centre of the battle and has continued to be the conservationists' headquarters.

This preoccupation with the environment has become important to many Tasmanians because they see it as the big hope for the future. The island state has transport problems that have discouraged the establishment of new labour-intensive industries and highlighted the importance of tourism. A battle has developed between the old order chasing industry and the new order intent on a utopia similar to the one the chocolate makers tried to create so many years ago.

Generally the people of Hobart have become more aware of what they have to offer, and they have gone out and started selling their unique lifestyle. After all, where else could a businessman in a capital city leave home at 8.45 a.m., start work at 9 a.m., knock off at 5 p.m., drive five minutes to a marina, jump in his yacht and cruise around the lower reaches of the Derwent, D'Entrecasteaux Channel and Storm Bay.

Suburban development pushes out to Bridgewater and beyond on the upper reaches of the Derwent. The rectangular grid patterns of the past have given way to the arcs and curves favoured by today's planners.

Above: *The Cadbury chocolate factory at Claremont and the adjacent golf links on Dogshear Point, north of the city.*

Right: *The beachside township of Kingston, south of the city towards the mouth of the Derwent River.*

It is one of the best cruising grounds in Australia, and attention centres on it each year as entrants in the Sydney–Hobart yacht race make their way to the finish line in Hobart. This race is one of the world's great bluewater classics. Up to 200 yachts leave Sydney every Boxing Day and head for the beautiful Constitution Dock, a couple of minutes' stroll from the centre of Hobart. The bulk of the fleet finishes before New Year's Day and gets a tremendous welcome from Hobart residents.

There is a party atmosphere on the docks as the New Year is welcomed in because the Sydney–Hobart, and more recently the Melbourne–Hobart, race finishes are the focal point for a Fiesta of diverse cultural and recreational activities. Salamanca Place, with one of the finest community arts centres in Australia, plays a big part in the Fiesta and visitors are impressed by the size and simplicity of the Saturday market. The sandstone buildings, century-old trees, music and buskers all combine to give a feeling of yesteryear.

The waterfront is the window of the city which, like most, is a combination of old and new. The old-established department stores compete against the trendier shopping centres, and the Elizabeth Mall gives shoppers a chance to rest and recuperate. But the river is all-powerful and when the sea breeze blows on summer afternoons it is the salt air, and not petrol fumes, that pervades the city centre.

An extension of the Hobart waterfront is the quaint suburb of Battery Point where the spire of St George's Anglican Church was a welcome sight for early mariners sailing up the river. The narrow winding streets and old buildings are an ideal setting for the art galleries, antique stores and restaurants that flourish here. Among them is Mure's, regarded as one of the finest seafood restaurants in Australia. Tasmania is renowned for its seafood and it is the ideal place to try the succulent crayfish, scallops, oysters and fresh scale fish like the deep sea trevalla. Mure's is one of many eating establishments in a city renowned for the number and quality of its restaurants.

A little further south is the suburb of Sandy Bay with its trendy boutiques and private schools — home of the wealthy. Close to the river are the old mansions and the old money. Further up the hill the views are more spectacular, the homes more modern and the overdrafts bigger. The suburb is a fitting host to Australia's first legalised casino: Wrest Point. The gamble was initially taken by Federal Hotels and the Tasmanian government in 1968 after a referendum indicated Tasmanians wanted a casino. Wrest Point, the redevelopment of an old international hotel, became a catalyst in the development of the state's tourist industry. In 1984 the convention and entertainment centre were added to the complex as it spread out over the river like some monstrosity from the set of *Star Wars*. In the Wrest Point gaming rooms one can enjoy gambling in its purest form: no garish poker machines line the walls to make a continual din; it is serious business. Apart from the odd nervous

Nowhere in Hobart is far from water, and swimming and water sports are popular summer activities. Hobart's beaches and coastal hideaways rarely suffer the congestion that mars those of larger cities.

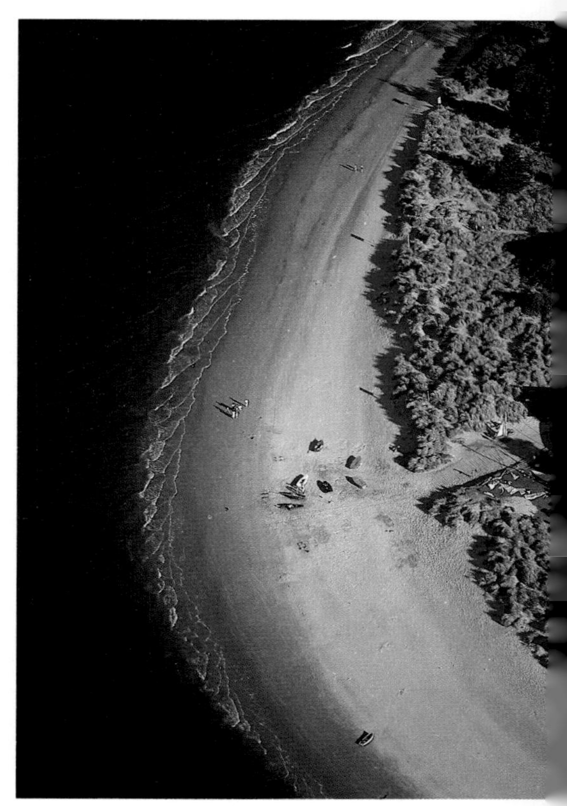

Above: *Hobart, the Southern Belle ringed by hills beyond which stretches the rich farmland of the Derwent valley.*

Left: *The 'peak minute' on the Tasman Bridge.*

giggle the sounds are few but necessary: the almost continuous roll of the ball around the roulette wheel, the dice bouncing in the cage, the click of the big lucky wheel and the monotonous call of the Keno numbers all add to the atmosphere.

It is standing room only at the tables on Friday and Saturday nights when the novice housewives rub shoulders with the interstate high rollers over for the weekend. The wheel spins and the $10 return for the $5 minimum bet on the first dozen leads to a squeal of delight from the uninitiated; the Sydney slicker does not hear as he checks through his pile of $50 chips, marks the number and colour down on his card, and continues to pursue his system.

The casino was the first legal one in Australia and is proof that Hobart residents can be innovative. After all Tattersalls started in Hobart and has flourished since moving to Melbourne and into the

Hobart by night: a city of sparkling lights, swirling patterns and still waters.

electronic age of Tattslotto. And the licensing laws are among the most liberal in the country: virtual around-the-clock trading hours for hotels were approved even before the casino opened its doors.

Predictions that the opening of the casino would lead to an upsurge in crime proved groundless. When it comes to nightlife the Southern Belle is fairly demure. There are few nightclubs and, apart from fairly discreet advertising from some escort agencies, there is little sign of after-dark adventures. Most activity centres on the casino and for a good night out Hobartians are content with a meal at one of the many excellent restaurants followed by a fling at the gaming tables.

Past Wrest Point the Derwent moves ponderously past the beachside suburbs of Kingston and Blackmans Bay — former seaside resorts where land has been snapped up as Hobart has expanded, and now a combination of tarted-up shacks and modern brick dwellings, they are linked to Hobart by the Southern Expressway.

And then the river finally joins the sea at the Iron Pot, where the lighthouse welcomes the weary mariner or yacht-race competitor looking for the annual New Year's Eve party, and farewells those who have enjoyed the renowned Hobart hospitality.

Above: *The Post Office tower and Town Hall dominate this view down Elizabeth Street towards the docks.*

Right: *The city lights, in a view upriver to the north.*

DAVID NASON

Pages 256–257: *Darwin's port area, looking towards the city centre.*

Left and below: *Central Darwin has been almost completely reconstructed after the damage wrought by Cyclone Tracy in December 1974. The modern Anglican cathedral incorporates a stone entrance, built in 1902 as the Lady Chapel for a future cathedral.*

Pages 260–261: *Wet-season clouds gather over Darwin Harbour, named by Captain J.C. Wickham in 1839 to honour Charles Darwin who had visited Australia as naturalist aboard the* Beagle *three years earlier.*

AUSTRALIA'S BEST-KEPT SECRET where the youthfulness and optimism is infectious; or an offbeat, Steinbeckian kind of outpost inhabited by beer-swilling eccentrics. These are varying impressions of Australia's northern capital, Darwin, made recently by visiting writers. Their words capture the energy and vitality that is typically Territorian but, more significantly, they illustrate the range of responses this tiny, isolated city can attract. This inability to pigeonhole Darwin has helped give it a mystique unmatched by Australia's other capital cities. Even today, in the age of international jet travel and satellite communications, Darwin remains to most Australians a confusing, even alien place somewhere on the periphery of the Outback. To be sure, it's a vision many suburban southerners find attractive — a preservation of the frontier traditions of old. It would have Darwin as some sort of lawless Dodge City where men fight first and talk about it over a beer later on. Perhaps there were elements of this cowboy romance in the Darwin of bygone days; but the Darwin that has emerged from the ruins wrought by Cyclone Tracy just over ten years ago is searching for a new identity, a new role in Australian affairs and a prosperity free from the charity of the past.

Distance probably more than any other factor has contributed to Darwin's historical isolation from the mainstream of Australian life. The closest state capital is Adelaide, a full 3620 kilometres 'down the track', and the Stuart Highway which connects them is still unsealed in some sections. The much-heralded Alice Springs–Darwin railway, promised by governments of all persuasion since 1911, is also yet to be built. Distance has made airline operations an essential service to Darwinites. The only practical way to get away for holidays is to fly, and despite prohibitive domestic airfares, thousands of Darwinites board south-bound planes from the city's ramshackle terminal each year. But many also board one of the three international airlines which operate out of Darwin and take holidays in nearby Asia. Cities like Singapore and Jakarta are not only closer to Darwin than Australia's capitals but are quite often connected by cheaper flights. Package holidays to Bali that are inexpensive by normal international standards are within the scope of even the most moderately paid worker and are extremely popular.

Distance has always been a factor preventing people coming to Darwin as well. Until comparatively recent times about the only newcomers seen in Darwin were public servants on one- and two-year transfers. Darwin was a government town to be sweated out until it was time to return to Melbourne or Sydney, hopefully with a promotion. These white-collar itinerants are probably responsible as much as anyone for Darwin's long-established reputation as the beer-drinking capital of the world. Tall tales of heroic drinking feats by government officials are a colourful part of local folklore. It led Xavier Herbert, celebrated author of classics like *Poor Fellow My Country* and *Capricornia*, to remark that Darwin's only exports were empty bottles and full public servants. But times have changed; people in Darwin still drink a lot, but more and more are deciding to settle down, build homes and raise families.

There are many reasons for this but the role of the humble air-conditioner should not be underestimated. It made the prospect of enduring the difficult early wet season months of October, November and December a whole lot easier for people accustomed to the gentle seasonal changes of southern states. These months generally record the highest humidity and in the days before air-conditioners the suicide rate during these periods seemed to rise with alarming regularity. Although nowadays statistics prove that such connections can't reasonably be drawn, people still talk of the 'suicide season' and 'going troppo'.

The monsoons which arrive in late December or early January bring relief with cloud cover that blocks out the sun and gentle winds. By April–May the rains are gone and the dry season — four or five months of the most invigorating outdoor-living weather to be found anywhere in the world — is underway. It's during these months that Darwinites traditionally defend their city and lifestyle with unrelenting vigour. And it's not hard to understand why: people can go swimming again (dangerous box jellyfish infest the water during the October–March wet-season months) and every imaginable water sport, bar surfing, is enjoyed; and at night, when the vast majority of Australians are sitting snug before an oil heater, Darwinites in shorts and T-shirts might be frying barramundi on a barbecue or taking a barefoot stroll on a moonlit beach. Banjo Paterson once wrote: 'A man who goes to the Territory always has a hankering to go back.' In Darwin it might well be said that a man who experiences a Top End dry season always has a hankering to return as well. The weather also gives rise to some curious sporting customs that are out of line with the rest of Australia: Australian Football, the major football code, is played in the wet season months; and cricket, the summer game, follows suit by playing in the dry season.

Right: *Part of the city. Following the havoc of Cyclone Tracy, new buildings must comply with rigid construction codes to help them withstand any similar future disaster.*

MLC

Darwin City: Looking along Smith Street with St Mary's Star of the Sea Catholic cathedral at bottom let (above left); *at work on the Darwin wharves* (far left); *the construction of the new Lower Court building* (left); *and a view towards the wharf area, showing, from left, Mitchell, Smith, Cavenagh and Woods Streets* (above).

But it takes more than good weather to make people put down roots thousands of kilometres from where they've grown up. In a nutshell Darwin is a boom town. There's a confidence in the future somehow free of the recession-influenced dismay of other cities. There's a belief that if you want to work hard almost anything is possible. There are countless stories of battlers who, with a little luck, a little cunning and a lot of sweat have cleaned up and gone into early retirement. Darwin's population figures tell their own story. With a population of nearly 64 000 Darwin is the fastest-growing city in Australia; it has expanded so fast that a satellite town, Palmerston, has been built 20 kilometres down the track. By the year 2000 Palmerston is expected to have 50 000 people while Darwin will have grown to 200 000; and these figures don't include the thousands of tourists expected to visit each year.

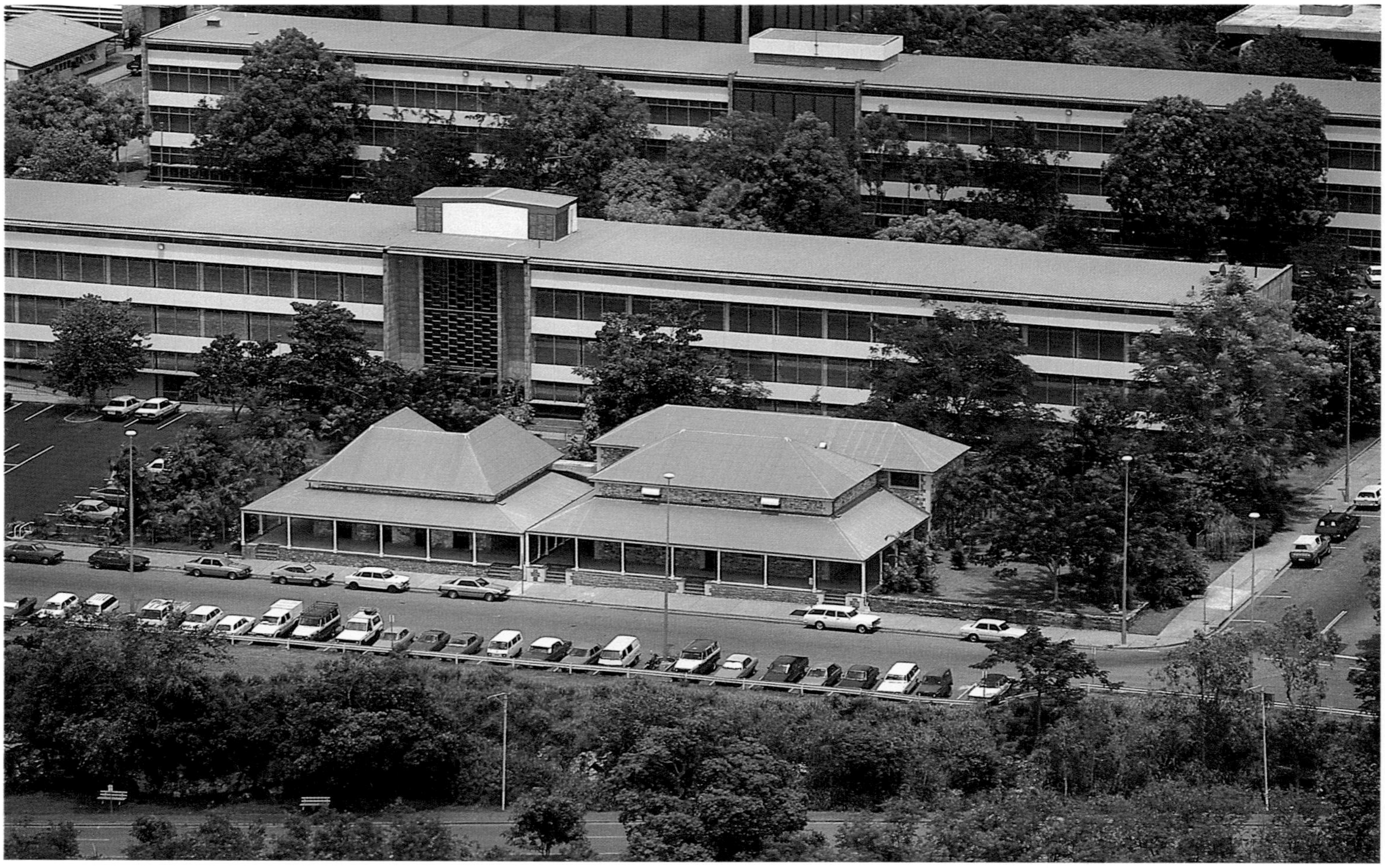

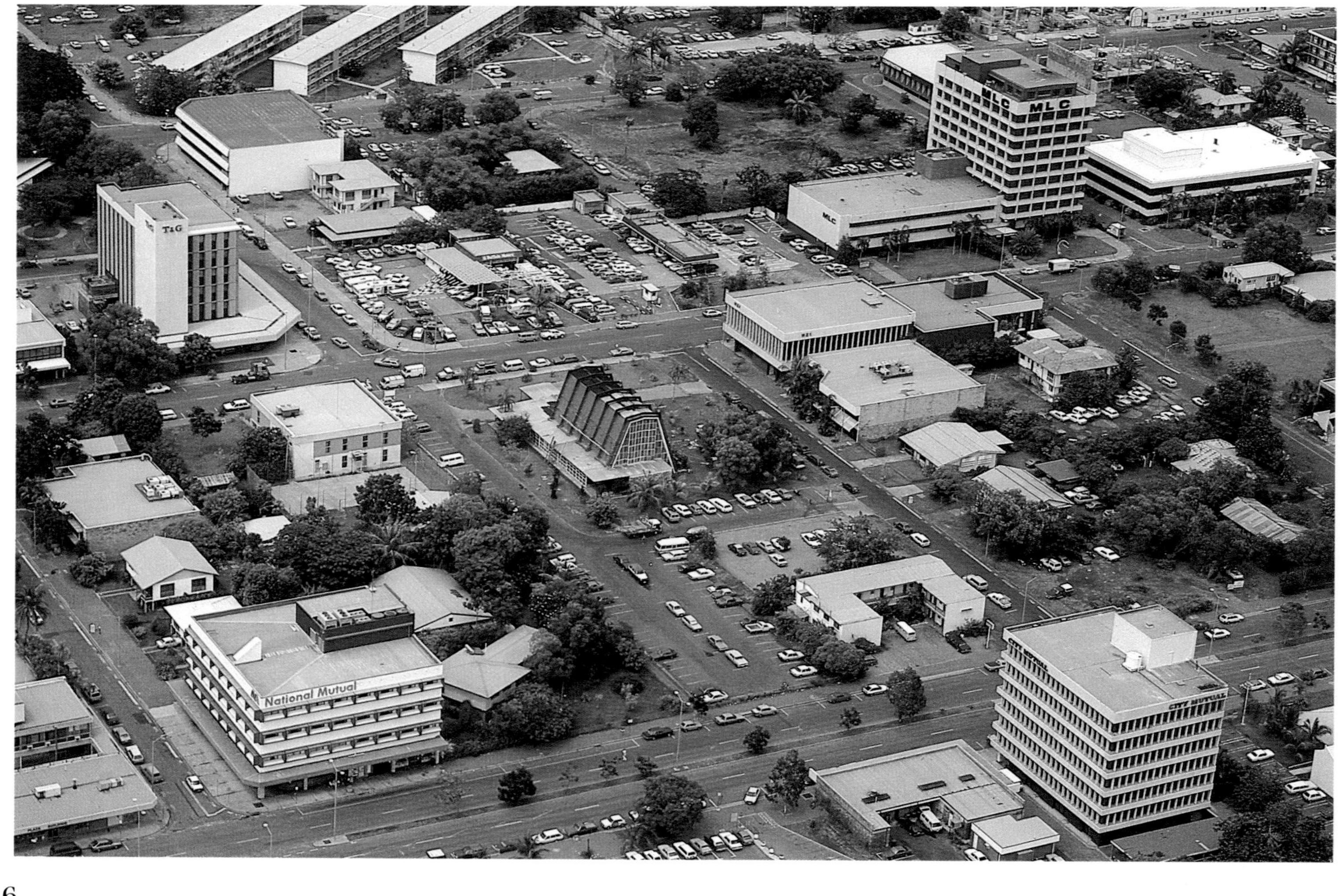
T&G
MLC
MLC
National Mutual

Above left: *The old Administrator's offices, with modern government administrative buildings behind.*

Left: *Looking towards the city: a view showing the Uniting church, commercial and government buildings.*

Above: *Darwin's Government House is a seven-gabled residence built in 1869, overlooking Darwin Harbour. Unlike most of Darwin's buildings, it has survived three cyclones and the bombing of World War II.*

Left: *City lights stretch over the flat peninsula on which Darwin is built.*

Right: *The Beaufort Centre for Performing Arts under construction, with the Travelodge to the right.*

Below: *Hostel accommodation, in the foreground, is provided for temporary postings in Darwin. The Diamond Beach casino can be seen in the background to the left.*

Much of Darwin's, indeed the Territory's, boom mentality is tied up in the almost religious belief that tourism can lead to a new era of prosperity. The Territory, and Darwin in particular, is tourist conscious. No longer are the inevitable busloads of wide-eyed visitors armed with cameras and wearing imitation slouch hats subjected to ridicule as was often the case in less enlightened times. There is a new respect for those previously looked upon as unwelcome, even foreign, intruders. And as a means of economic salvation tourism has been embraced with equal passion by both sides in the Territory's home of government, the Legislative Assembly. Territory politicians say the industry is labour intensive and will solve problems of unemployment. They say the Territory has the natural wonders to attract tourists in large droves, especially from Asia. And all around investors are agreeing with them and putting up money for the construction of a bigger and better tourism infrastructure. In Darwin several big hotels are under construction and more are planned. The city has already developed a sophisticated and vibrant nightlife centred around the casino built on Mindil Beach, just a short distance from town. The casino, with its coloured lights and temple-like grandeur, symbolises the new aspirations of the city — aspirations which no longer centre on preserving Darwin's isolationism and local character at the expense of everything else. The new Darwin, just like the new Territory, is opening the door, especially in Asia, and welcoming everybody in. The transformation is all that much more amazing when one considers that a little over ten years ago in Darwin there was hardly a door left standing.

Port Darwin is situated in an extensive natural harbour, with a considerable tidal variation which enables it to handle large vessels. As the central distribution point for the 'Top End', it exports meat, minerals, iron ore and prawns, and imports building materials, petroleum and consumer goods.

The Diamond Beach casino on Mindil Beach (left, background), *a building of 'temple-like grandeur', is both a centre of Darwin's more sophisticated nightlife and a symbol of the city's aspirations to become an international tourist destination.*

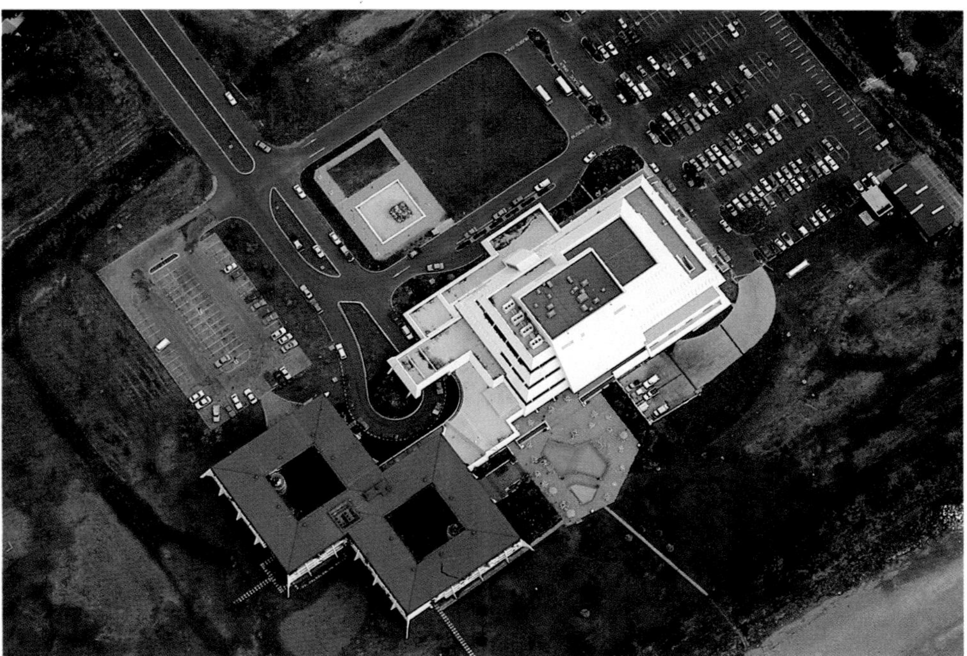

People have called Darwin Australia's lucky city. There is, in fact, good reason to call it the unluckiest. No other Australian city has endured three catastrophes of the magnitude of the bombing by the Japanese in 1942 and the cyclones of 1937 and Christmas Day, 1974. Three times in the last fifty years the city has been on its knees; each time there were calls to abandon it; but each time the people of Darwin refused to give in and the city grew again. After Cyclone Tracy unleashed her fury on Darwin on the morning of 25 December 1974, many thought she was not worth rebuilding. But the people of Darwin rallied and with typical determination — and a lot of Commonwealth money — the flattened city picked itself up from the canvas. Virtually the whole city was rebuilt from scratch making Darwin by far the most modern of all Australia's capitals.

East Point. The gun turrets date from World War II when they were installed as protection against an expected Japanese invasion. Although the feared land invasion did not occur, a Japanese air raid on 19 February 1942 caused hundreds of deaths and extensive damage to the city.

Perhaps the most amazing part of Darwin's rise after Tracy has been the regrowth of the decimated vegetation. Hardly a tree or bush was left standing after Tracy had plundered through and those that remained upright were shredded of foliage. Today it seems a miracle has taken place: a veritable riot of tropical growth has followed a deliberate plan by the city's planners formulated in the wake of the cyclone; the city is a garden of towering palms, flaming bougainvilleas and ferns of a hundred different varieties. A lot of the credit must go to Darwin City Council Parks and Gardens officer George Brown; he has supervised this greening of Darwin and nowhere is his work more luxuriant than the city's glorious Botanical Gardens. But it's out in the sprawling suburbia Darwinites call simply the Northern Suburbs that the true value of the greening campaign is being realised. The newly built suburbs surrounded, sometimes engulfed, by undergrowth have managed to avoid the cold spartan feel of similar working-class areas in Australia's other cities. It is still suburbia, yes, but that's something that can't be avoided. Darwin's tropical suburbia, with each home a potential oasis, gives hope that a peaceful stimulating home environment can be enjoyed by all.

Right: *Casuarina Olympic Pool and shopping centre.*

Below: *A new-style caravan park with private facilities and, behind, part of Darwin's ever-expanding suburbia, petering out on its fringes to the flat country of the 'Top End'.*

MASTER LOCKSMITH
Kmart

Above and right: *The Darwin suburb of Nightcliff.*

Above and right: *The satellite town of Palmerston, twenty kilometres from Darwin city. Palmerston's growth is witness to Darwin's confidence about its future development and prosperity.*

I come now to what makes Darwin unique in Australia ahead of all else and what makes it truly a lucky city. In the 1981 census 100 overseas locations were recorded as birthplaces by 22.3 per cent of Territorians. It means one in every three non-Aboriginal residents (Aborigines comprise 25 per cent of the Northern Territory population) is overseas born. The largest ethnic group is probably the Greeks with about 7000 but there are large numbers of Chinese, Italians, Dutch, Timorese, Germans and New Zealanders. In short Darwin is a cosmopolitan melting pot of just about every race, creed and colour imaginable. And the fact that all these people can get on well together without the tensions and rivalry that characterise so many other places where people of different backgrounds are thrown together is Darwin's most endearing quality. It seems to make a lie of Australia's reputation for racial intolerance to see a former Greek taxi driver, Nick Dondas, as deputy leader of the CLP government and a third-generation Chinaman, Alec Fong Lim, as Lord Mayor. Darwin accepts this with its usual casual indifference to matters of ethnic origin. Why this has happened I cannot say: perhaps it's the result of Darwin's long history of racial interaction; perhaps Darwin, because of its location, has remained isolated from the prejudices which afflict different people all over the world; perhaps it's because no one ethnic group controls the majority of the wealth of the city.

Whatever the reason, Darwin's racial harmony is its most attractive quality. More and more people are discovering it contributes in a tangible way to a more stimulating environment where the customs and traditions of one may be enjoyed by all. Australia may no longer be the lucky country but way up north, on the other side of the Outback, a place called Darwin has somehow found a peace which might well be a model for cities everywhere.

ACKNOWLEDGMENTS

The publishers would like to thank the staff
of the government tourist bureaus of Victoria, Queensland, Western Australia, South Australia, the Northern Territory and the Australian Capital Territory for their assistance and advice in the preparation of this book.

Grateful acknowledgment is also made to the management and pilots of the Channel 7 Network who assisted in the provision of the helicopters from which many of the photographs were taken.

NOTES ON PHOTOGRAPHY

Most images in this book were photographed with Mamiya R2 6x7 cm cameras and 50 mm, 65 mm, 110 mm and 250 mm lenses, supplied by Sam Lewis Photographics, Sydney.

Close-up images were recorded with Nikon 35 mm cameras and lenses. The 180 mm f2.8 ED and the 300 mm f2.8 IF-ED proved to be particularly useful.

For the gatefolds and some of the double-spread images a Sinar Handy camera with 65 mm and 120 mm Schneider lenses with 6x12 cm and 4 in x 5 in film magazines provided correction of perspective distortion.

Films used were 120 Fujichrome RDP and 35 mm Kodachrome PKR. All photographs were taken without gyro-stabilisers.

NOTES ON CONTRIBUTORS

KEITH DUNSTAN

Keith Dunstan began his distinguished career in journalism in 1949, as a newspaper columnist in New York and London. Since then his columns in newspapers and magazines have been written from Melbourne, Brisbane and the West Coast of the United States. He is the author of several books on Australian social mores, including **Wowsers, Knockers, Sports, Ratbags** *and* **Saint Ned.** *An avowed lover of Melbourne, Dunstan was the founder of the Anti-Football League and one-time president of the Melbourne Press Club and Bicycle Institute of Victoria.*

ROBERT HAUPT

Robert Haupt is a reporter and interviewer on the Nine Network's 'Sunday' program, and a newspaper columnist. He is the author of **Thirty-one Days to Power**, *an account of the election of Bob Hawke. Haupt first went to Canberra in 1968 as a reporter covering parliament. After spells in Washington as a correspondent for the* **Financial Review**, *and Melbourne, as assistant editor of the* **Age**, *he now lives in Sydney and visits Canberra for parliamentary sittings.*

CHRIS MILNE

Chris Milne is an Adelaide-based journalist, senior feature writer for the **Advertiser**. *He was born in the city, a couple of hundred metres from the Adelaide Oval scoreboard designed by a great-uncle. The parklands and the River Torrens banks were his childhood playground. He has left Adelaide twice to live overseas, the second time for almost four years as European correspondent for Australian newspapers, and travels whenever possible. But he enjoys returning to the comfortable convenience of his home town, where he now lives with his wife – a school bus driver — his four children and a parrot-infested almond tree.*

HUGH LUNN

Hugh Lunn was born in Brisbane forty-four years ago. From 1964 to 1971 he worked overseas for Reuters Newsagency in London, Saigon, Singapore and Jakarta. Since returning home he has won three Walkley awards for the best feature writing in Australia. He has also won a National Press Club award for the best sporting feature in Australia. His three books, **Joh, Behind the Banana Curtain** *and* **Queenslanders**, *have all been well received, with* **Joh** *reaching number two on the national best-seller list. For the past fifteen years, Hugh Lunn has represented the* **Australian** *newspaper in Brisbane.*

NANCY KEESING

Nancy Keesing is a poet, general writer and critic. Born in Sydney in 1923, she has lived near its harbour for most of her life. She was educated at SCEGGS, Darlinghurst, and Frensham, Mittagong, and Sydney University. She has been active in writers' affairs and was chairman of the Literature Board of the Australia Council from 1974 to 1977. Her publications include four books of poetry; two historical novels for children; a memoir; biography; collections of **Australian Bush Ballads** *and* **Old Bush Songs** *(with Douglas Stewart); numerous anthologies; and, most recently,* **Lily on the Dustbin** *(Penguin 1982),* **Just Look Out the Window** *(Penguin 1985) and* **Dear Mum** *(Angus & Robertson 1985).*

ROSS GATES

Ross Gates has spent most of his working life in Hobart and is currently the day news editor of Tasmania's only metropolitan newspaper, the **Mercury**. *Away from the office he spends time playing golf, sailing and swimming, which is why he has a great love and understanding of the lifestyle of Hobart. He is married with two daughters.*

DAVID NASON

David Nason is a journalist who first went to Darwin from his native South Australia in 1977 to play football. Like many southerners, he soon found the easy-paced lifestyle attractive and, apart from a few short breaks interstate and seven months in Alice Springs, he has remained to become one of those curious creatures known as Darwinites. He has watched with awe and sadness as a seemingly endless range of development projects change the face of Darwin, bringing a degree of big-city intensity at odds with the city's traditionally casual lifestyle. These days David Nason is chief of staff at Darwin's daily newspaper, the **Northern Territory News**. *He still plays football, never wears a tie, and likes to watch the sun set over Fannie Bay.*

HUGH SCHMITT

Hugh Schmitt, who started a cadetship with the Perth **Daily News** *in 1947, later became chief of staff of that paper for six years. After an eleven year stint as director of the Perth News Bureau, he was appointed special representative in New York for the Herald & Weekly Times group. Now, after three and half years in New York, he is a special features writer on the* **West Australian**. *In 1983 he won the H.B. Jackson Memorial Prize for the best piece of creative or analytical writing.*

INDEX

This index lists places, monuments and buildings mentioned in the captions and featured in the photographs to which they refer.